INTRODUCTION TO DWARF HAMSTERS

Dwarf hamsters are extraordinary animals. Soft-furred, bright-eyed, and lively, these minuscule charmers make delightful pets. There are four dwarf hamster species kept as pets. They have individual personalities, amazing abilities, unique adaptations, and special needs. The tiny dwarf hamster has a big story to tell!

What Is a Dwarf Hamster?

Dwarf hamsters are small mammals native to the exotic and arid desert regions of northern China, Manchuria, Mongolia, and Siberia. Dwarf hamsters are not a variety, breed, or miniature version of the more common and much larger Golden Syrian hamster. There are several species of dwarf hamsters. Each species is different in size, appearance, behavior, and reproduction.

The word *hamster* is derived from the German word *hamstern*, meaning to hoard. Food hoarding is an instinctive survival behavior characteristic of all hamster species (there are more than twenty-five species). Hoarding helps hamsters to survive during times when food is scarce.

Dwarf hamsters originate from regions consisting mostly of dry plains, stiff grasses, and sand dunes, so they are often referred to as "desert hamsters." Dwarf hamsters are also called "pocket pets." This is simply a term for companion animals so tiny they *could* fit in a pocket—it does not mean they should be put or kept in a pocket!

The four dwarf hamster species that are kept as pets are the Djungarian hamster (*Phodopus campbelli*), commonly known as the Campbell's hamster; the Siberian hamster (*Phodopus sungorus*), commonly called the Winter White hamster; the Desert hamster (*Phodopus roborovskii*), commonly referred to as the Roborovskii hamster; and the Chinese hamster (*Cricetulus griseus*).

As you have just noted, dwarf hamsters have many different names. In fact, as you will learn in this book, dwarf hamsters have several mores names than those just mentioned. Many of these names have been used interchangeably for the different species. This has caused considerable confusion ever since these tiny animals were first discovered. Throughout this book we use the common names that are accepted as correct and that are used by scientists, zoologists, and mammalogists in research laboratories, and in scientific publications.

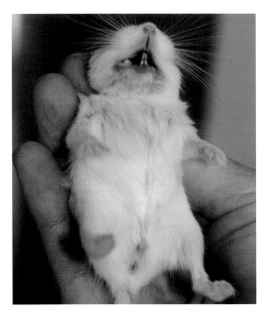

Dwarf hamsters have a mid-ventral scent gland located in the center of the abdomen. The scent gland may stain the surrounding fur yellow. This is normal.

These names are also recognized by the American Society of Mammalogists. These are: Djungarian hamster, Siberian hamster, Desert hamster, and Chinese hamster. To avoid confusion, we also include the names used by pet fanciers and pet stores. These are Campbell's hamster, Winter White hamster, Roborovskii hamster, and Chinese hamster, respectively. For additional clarification, the scientific names, genus and species, are often included.

Different species of dwarf hamsters may look similar, but they are very different in social behavior, personality, biology, housing needs, reproduction, and genetics. We discuss each of the dwarf hamster species in detail throughout this book.

Hamster Characteristics

Dwarf hamsters are very attractive animals. Their large heads, bright eyes, small noses, long whiskers, and soft fur give them a cuddly appearance. The rounded ears are protected by a lining of hair on the inside surface; these teddy-bear ears give the hamster a soft expression. The compact body and short tail add to its appeal.

Eyes: Although hamsters have large eyes, they do not see well. The placement of their eyes, on the side of the head, compensates to a certain degree for this deficiency. It gives the hamster a wide range of vision out of each eye, making it possible for the hamster to see predators approaching from all directions: front, sides, above, and somewhat behind. It is an anatomical adaptation for survival.

Bodies: Hamsters have strong shoulders and stocky, robust bodies. They are excellent diggers and can move amazing quantities of material in a short period of time. A hamster's body is extremely flexible so it is able to enter the tiniest spaces.

Legs and feet: Hamsters are excellent climbers and fast runners. Their short legs are remarkably strong. The front legs are stronger than the back legs. Hamster feet are short and broad. There are four toes and claws on each of the front feet, plus a *vestigial thumb* (a small bump where a thumb usually exists in other animals). There are five toes on the rear feet. Unlike other hamsters, some dwarf hamsters have densely haired feet.

Skin: Hamster skin fits very loosely, providing an excellent defense mechanism. A frightened or threatened hamster is able to turn in its skin and bite just about anything or anyone that has a hold on it.

Cheek pouches: An interesting anatomical feature of hamsters is the internal cheek pouches, which are used to collect and transport huge quantities of food and nesting material. The cheek pouches are located on both sides of the face, near the angle of the mouth. They can be filled to such capacity that the animal's disfigured appearance can be startling. The cheek pouches can enlarge to one third the size of the hamster's entire body and extend over the shoulders. They can even interfere with shoulder movement. New hamster owners unfamiliar with this amazing hamster adaptation often mistake it for a disease, such as mumps. But the pouches do not remain full for long. Hamsters are busy animals that love to forage, collect, transport, and hoard. When ready to empty the cheek pouches, or when disturbed, the hamster uses its forepaws to push the contents from the back of the cheek pouches forward, while at the same time opening its mouth very wide, appearing to yawn. When this happens, the contents of the cheek pouches pour out.

Whiskers: Hamsters are well adapted for their underground and nighttime (nocturnal) activities. One of the hamster's most important adaptive features is its very long *vibrissae,* or whiskers. Vibrissae are located on the face and on the sides of the body. They serve to guide the hamster by sense of touch. Hamsters rely heavily on their vibrissae to guide them and prevent them from falling off objects or bumping into things. Vibrissae are vital to hamsters, whether they are exploring during the daylight hours or navigating the dark interior of nests

Dwarf hamsters stand out as one of the most interesting of the 1,814 rodent species.

and dens. The location of the vibrissae varies for each hamster species and plays an important role in individual behavioral characteristics.

Sense of smell: What the hamster lacks in vision is compensated for by its extraordinary sense of smell. Hamsters depend on their noses to lead them to food and water, warn them of danger, identify other animals, find their homes, and to tell them the right time to breed. In fact, odor is so important to hamsters that they have special scent glands on their bodies. These scent glands produce a musklike odor. They are used to create sexual attraction, to mark and identify territories, and as a means of recognizing each other. Depending on the species, scent glands may be located on the face, cheek pouches, behind the ears, in the center of the belly (mid-ventral scent glands), and on each flank. The flank scent glands are

Dwarf hamsters originate from arid regions in Russia, China, and Mongolia.

larger in males than in females and are influenced by sex hormones. In the male, these darkly pigmented areas are surrounded by dark, bristly hairs; the hair surrounding the smaller flank scent glands in the female are softer. Hamsters spend a lot of time grooming the area around their scent glands.

Hearing: Hamsters have excellent hearing and are able to hear a wide range of sounds. Studies have shown that hamsters can communicate in the ultrasonic range. Even baby hamsters call to their mothers in this range. This is an amazing protective mechanism—the ability to communicate with each other without being heard by every predator.

What Makes Hamsters Rodents?

Dwarf hamsters are rodents. To better understand your pet's habits, personality, instincts, and special needs it helps to know just what a rodent is. Rodents are among the most diverse and numerous of mammalian species. Among the more than 2,000 species of rodents, dwarf hamsters stand out to many hobbyists and researchers as some of the most intriguing of them all.

Rodents are classified according to anatomical characteristics, similarities in teeth and bone structure, origin, and lifestyle. All rodents have two upper and two lower front teeth (incisors). Growth of the incisors takes place at the base of the tooth and continues throughout the animals' lives. To prevent the teeth from becoming too long, hamsters constantly grind their teeth and chew on hard materials. This instinctive behavior keeps the teeth worn to an appropriate and functional length. Continual wear of the incisors maintains very sharp cutting surfaces.

Rodents do not have canine teeth or anterior (front) premolars, so there is a large space between the front teeth and the cheek teeth.

This space, called the *diastema,* is filled with a velvety fold of skin. The cheek teeth, or molars, are located at the back of the mouth. Although they are not easy to see when the hamster opens its mouth, there are twelve molars, three above and three below on each side of the mouth. The molars are used for grinding hard foods, such as grains. Molars have peculiar surface patterns, which together with teeth alignment and jaw structure, help scientists determine how different rodent species developed over time, their relationship to each other, and their origin.

Their Place in Nature

Animals, insects, and plants are classified and grouped according to their differences and similarities. Names are assigned according to kingdom, phylum, class, order, family, genus, and species. With each progressive category, animals grouped together are more closely related. For example, all animals are part of the Kingdom Animalia, but only rodents are members of the Order Rodentia. The dwarf hamsters are grouped with more closely related rodents, such as other hamsters, and belong to the Family Muridae.

The name given to a class, order, family, genus, or species may come from different sources. Animals can be named according to a special characteristic of their group, named after the person who discovered them, or even named after the geographical area they naturally inhabit.

As we continue to learn more about the life forms around us, there is sometimes a need to make changes or revisions in the way we have categorized certain animal groups. This is especially true for dwarf hamsters. Over the cen-

turies, they have been named, renamed, and reclassified. In fact, different hamster species used to share the same names! To help avoid confusion, we will review how dwarf hamsters are classified and named today, as well as their classification and assigned names in past years.

Dwarf Hamster Classification

The dwarf hamster is a member of the Kingdom Animalia (Animal Kingdom), the Phylum Chordata (animals having spinal columns), and the Class Mammalia (mammals). The word *mammalia* refers to mammary glands (mammae, teats, or breasts). Newborn and baby mammals are nourished by milk from their mothers' breasts. All warm-blooded animals with hair or fur that have mammary glands belong to the Class Mammalia.

Order Rodentia: The word *Rodentia* is derived from the Latin word *rodere,* which means "to gnaw." This is a reference to the continual need of all rodents to chew. The most important characteristic shared by all rodents is the continual growth of their front teeth throughout their entire lives. Within the Order Rodentia, the dwarf hamster belongs to the Suborder Sciurognathia, Superfamily Muroidea, Family Muridea, and Subfamily Cricetinae.

There are two genera of dwarf hamsters: Genus *Phodopus* and Genus *Cricetulus.*

Genus Phodopus: The word *Phodopus* comes from the Greek words *phodos,* meaning "blister" or "tubercle," and *pous,* meaning "foot." The description of a "blister foot" refers to the appearance of the bottom of the animals' feet. The footpads on each foot are all fused together, so that there appears to be only one, large, bumpy footpad. Species in Genus *Phodopus* are *campbelli* (Djungarian hamster), *roborovskii* (Desert hamster), and *sungorus* (Siberian hamster).

Genus Cricetulus: This genus has only one species kept as pocket pets, *Cricetulus griseus.* Species are identified by the first letter of the genus name, followed by the species name. The four dwarf hamsters we discuss are *C. griseus, P. campbelli, P. roborovskii,* and *P. sungorus.*

The Different Species

✔ The Djungarian hamster (*Phodopus campbelli*)

✔ The Siberian hamster (*Phodopus sungorus*)

✔ The Roborovskii Hamster (*Phodopus roborovskii*)

✔ The Chinese hamster (*Cricetulus griseus*)

Each rodent species is unique in its genetic makeup, biology, and behavior; yet, some species are so closely related and so similar in appearance that they can be identified only by experts. For example, for many years the Djungarian hamster and the Siberian hamster were believed to be the same species. This is not surprising, as the two species closely resemble each other and may be found in the same regions.

Dwarf Hamster Names Throughout the Centuries

Present Scientific Name	Name origin	First described	First scientific names
Phodopus campbelli	Named after W. C. Campbell, who found and collected a specimen in Mongolia July 1, 1902	1905 by Thomas	*Cricetulus campbelli*; Thomas 1905 *Phodopus crepidatus*; Hollister 1912 *Phodopus campbelli*; Hollister 1912 *Cricetiscus campbelli*; Thomas 1917
Phodopus sungorus	Named according to physical traits	1773 by Pallas	*Mus sungorus*; Pallas 1773 *Mus songarus*; Pallas 1778 *Phodopus sungorus*; Hollister 1912
Phodopus roborovskii	Named after Lieutenant Roborovskii, who discovered the species in 1894	1903 by Satunin	*Cricetulus roborovskii*; Satunin 1903 *Cricetulus bedfordiae*; Thomas 1908 *Phodopus praedilectus*; Mori 1930
Cricetulus griseus	Named according to physical traits and color	1773 by Pallas	*Cricetulus barabensis*; Pallas 1773 *Barabensis griseus*; 1857 Milne-Edwards

Because Djungarian and Siberian hamsters were originally believed to be one and the same species, various common names for them were used interchangeably. Names like *striped hairy-footed hamster,* Zjungarian hamster, Zungarian hamster, Dzungarian hamster, Djungarian hamster, Siberian hamster, Russian hamster, Dwarf Winter White hamster, Desert hamster, and *Phodopus* were all general terms used to describe these animals.

To complicate matters more, early researchers could not decide on the most suitable scientific names for hamsters in the *Phodopus* genus and changed the names several times. This is a good

Dwarf Hamster Facts

Name	Djungarian hamster	Siberian hamster
Common name	Campbell's hamster	Winter White hamster
Scientific name	*Phodopus campbelli*	*Phodopus sungorus*
Other names	Dwarf Russian hamster, Eastern Russian hamster	Dwarf Russian hamster, striped hairy-footed hamster, Western Russian hamster
Origin	Central Asia, Mongolia, Northern China, Southern Siberia	Kazakhstan, Manchuria, Mongolia, Siberia
Color (color found naturally in the wild)	Gray–brown to light gray on back, ivory on sides, white on abdomen	Gray back, white abdomen, dark line separating gray and white fur (the "triple arch line"), color is almost entirely white in winter
Markings	Thin, dark gray stripe down back, ends 1 inch (2.5 cm) above base of tail; variety of colors	Thick, black stripe down back that extends to base of tail; dark patch on head; also found in a few other colors in captivity
Body shape	Stocky, compact, less-rounded back	Short, robust, compact, rounded back
Body length	3 to 4 inches (7.6 to 10 cm)	4 inches (10 cm)
Head shape	Head shorter and less deep than *P. sungorus*; eyes placed equal distance between ears and nose; broad nose	Head longer and deeper than *P. campbelli*; convex face; large eyes set closer to ears than to nose
Weight	1 ounce (28.35 g)	1 to 2 ounces (28.35 to 56.70 g)
Scent glands	Mid-ventral scent glands, cheek pouch secretory saccules, scent glands in skin behind the ears	Mid-ventral scent gland, cheek pouch secretory saccules
Easiest to handle and tame	Sometimes quick and also the most likely to bite	Easy to handle, slow, sluggish, easy to tame
Social and breeding behavior	Biparental: Father's help raising pups is very important to their survival; easy to breed and raise in captivity; enjoys companionship and group housing	Uniparental: Father helps raise pups but his help is not necessary for pup survival; easy to breed and raise in captivity; enjoys companionship and group housing
Most active	February, March, early evening, twilight	November, evening; can conserve energy in cold conditions by torpor
Least active	November	February, March
Life span	1$\frac{1}{2}$ to 2 years	1$\frac{1}{2}$ to 2 years

Desert hamster	Chinese hamster
Roborovskii hamster	Chinese hamster
Phodopus roborovskii	*Cricetulus griseus*
Dwarf Russian hamster, robby, robo	Ratlike hamster, striped hamster, striped-back hamster, grey hamster
China, Mongolia, Russia	China
Sandy shades from brown to brown–apricot	Gray to gray–brown, with light gray abdomen
No stripe down back; white patch above each eye	Dark stripe down back; dark patch on crown of head; some individuals may have white spots
Stocky, compact, rounded back	Long, slim, robust; similar to a rat
2 inches (5.1 cm)	4 to 5 inches (10 to 13 cm)
Broad head, rounded when viewed from the back; large eyes	Elongated head with blunt muzzle; eyes placed almost equal distance between ears and nose
$1/2$ to $3/4$ ounce (14 to 21 g)	1 to $1^1/2$ ounces (28 to 42 g)
Mid-ventral scent glands	Mid-ventral scent glands, flank scent glands
Challenging to handle, quick and jumpy	Easy to handle, friendly toward people
Easy to breed and raise in captivity; can be colonial and enjoys group housing	Most difficult to breed and raise in captivity; often prefers solitary housing; very aggressive toward other hamsters
November, late evenings	Spring, summer, day, night
February, March	Fall, winter
3 to $3^1/2$ years	2 to 3 years

thing, because the Siberian hamster (*Phodopus sungorus*) was initially misclassified in 1773 as a mouse species (*Mus*)!

Scientists later learned that the Siberian hamster and the Djungarian hamster differed in many ways. They decided that the two animals were not the same species, and considered the Djungarian hamster to be a subspecies of the Siberian hamster. The Siberian hamster was then referred to as *Phodopus sungorus sungorus* and the Djungarian hamster was referred to as *Phodopus sungorus campbelli*.

Scientific research has now clearly demonstrated that the Siberian hamster, *Phodopus sungorus*, and the Djungarian hamster, *Phodopus campbelli*, are indeed two separate and distinct species. Note: The middle name, *sungorus*, has been deleted from both names.

A third species of *Phodopus* hamster is *Phodopus roborovskii*, the Desert hamster. This name is also confusing, because all the dwarf hamsters have been called desert hamsters in the past. Add to the confusion the Chinese hamster, *Cricetulus griseus*. Even though it is in a completely different genus, and does not look like the *Phodopus* hamsters, it has shared their name, the striped hamster.

Dwarf hamster nomenclature (system of names) for scientific and common names is confusing and complicated. It is no wonder that when you read older literature about dwarf hamsters it is often difficult to know which species is actually being discussed. Unfortunately, even today, many recent books, hamster Web sites, and Internet sources continue to use incorrect nomenclature for different hamster species.

When you read about dwarf hamsters in various publications, keep in mind that the Djungarian hamster is often called the Campbell's

hamster and the Siberian hamster is often called the Winter White hamster. The name Winter White is misleading, as the Siberian hamster is only white part of the year and only under certain conditions. Even then, the Siberian hamster usually retains some color, especially on its head. The Desert hamster is often called the Roborovskii hamster. Fortunately, everyone calls the Chinese hamster "the Chinese hamster"!

Now you know the past, present, common, and scientific names for the four pet dwarf hamster species. Whenever you are discussing or writing about a specific species, rather than dwarf hamsters in general, you can avoid confusion by using the animals' genus and species names.

The Djungarian Hamster, *Phodopus campbelli* (Campbell's Russian Hamster)

History: Dwarf hamsters, like *most* rodents sold as pets today, descend from ancestors that were captured in the wild. These wild distant relatives were first raised in captivity in research laboratory colonies, established in the early 1900s to study the animals' biology. Today's pet dwarf hamster is hundreds of generations removed from those first, few original captive animals.

The first laboratory colony of Djungarian hamsters was established in Leningrad by the Zoological Institute of the Academy of Sciences of the Soviet Union. The colony was created with a group of hamsters captured in Tuva, in Mongolia. Later, one female hamster and two male hamsters were taken from the Leningrad colony and sent to the Institute of Experimental and Clinical Oncology in Moscow. These animals produced young that were in turn exported and used to start laboratory research colonies in parts of Europe. With its endearing personality and fascinating behavior, it didn't take long to recognize the Djungarian hamster's potential as a popular pocket pet, and this charming creature soon found its way into the homes and hearts of the general public. It is now the most commonly available dwarf hamster in pet stores.

Description: The Djungarian hamster is named after one of the regions it inhabits, Djungaria (or Dzungaria), Mongolia. It is also found in parts of northern China, central Asia, and Russia.

The adult male hamster is slightly larger than the female, measuring 3 to 4 inches (7.6 to 10 cm) from nose to rump and weighing about 1 to 1½ ounces (28 to 42 g). An adult female measures up to 3½ inches (9 cm) in length and weighs approximately 1 ounce (30 g). The tail is very short, about ¼ of an inch (10 mm) in length, and is usually tucked away, hidden in the fur. The female has four pairs of mammary glands (eight teats).

Raising Djungarian hamsters has become a popular hobby. Many hamster breeders have established genetic lines of dwarf hamsters with a variety of coat colors, patterns, and textures (see Breeding for Coat Colors and Textures, page 101), but most pet Djungarian hamsters are colored like those observed in the wild. These attractive animals are gray on the head, back, and sides, with creamy buff fur on the belly, throat, and underparts. The buff coloration extends from the hamster's underside up onto the shoulders, sides, and hips, making three attractive curved patch designs. The undercoat is gray and there is a narrow, dark brown or black stripe that extends from the nape of the neck to about 1 inch (2.5 cm)

above the base of the tail. The mouth and cheeks are creamy buff in color and the tops of the densely furred feet are silvery white.

Natural habitat and diet: In its natural environment, the Djungarian hamster prefers solid ground to sand dunes. It can be found in areas where there are mud flats and clay soil. Here it is able to dig the several horizontal and vertical tunnels that lead to its burrows. Some of the tunnels can be as deep as 2 to 3 feet (61 to 91 cm). The hamster lines its nesting burrows with suitable material found in the area, usually dry grass and sheep wool. The temperature inside the burrow is warm (62°F [16.7°C]) compared to the outside temperature ranges (–5°F to 72°F [–25°C to +23°C]).

Having access to several tunnels can be life-saving—there are various hamster predators in Mongolia; the most dangerous are foxes, owls, falcons, and weasels. Deep tunnels and warm bedding material are necessary for the hamster to successfully raise its young because

Quick and nimble, the tiny Roborovskii hamster is half the size of other dwarf hamsters. It has an attractive white patch above each eye and it lacks a dorsal stripe.

Djungarian hamsters do not tolerate the cold as well as other dwarf hamsters do.

During the evenings the Djungarian hamster can travel as far as a mile foraging for food. Its diet varies according to the season and grain availability, and is made up mostly of insects and seeds. Insects are an important source of moisture for the Djungarian hamster, especially in times of drought.

Behavior: Djungarian hamsters, like other *Phodopus* hamsters, are active at night. They are also active during the twilight hours, especially around 6:00 P.M. This twilight activity is

A Siberian hamster celebrates summer in its dark gray coat and white belly.

called *crepuscular activity*. The word *crepuscular* comes from the French word *crépuscule*, which means "twilight." It is also active throughout the year, being most active during the month of February. When it isn't foraging, scent-marking, or arranging its nest, this fastidious animal is certain to be grooming itself.

Hamsters can be fast runners, but compared to some dwarf hamsters the Djungarian hamster seems a bit lazy and is a slow mover. It also does not seem to be as disturbed by bright lights or the presence of people. This makes it easy to capture or observe.

Both male and female parents are active participants in raising a family. Scientists believe this shared biparental behavior has a lot to do with keeping the baby hamsters, called "pups," warm during their development (see Raising Dwarf Hamsters, page 79).

Special characteristics: The Djungarian hamster has adapted well to its desert lifestyle. Its expandable cheek pouches are used for transporting large amounts of food and material to use in times of need. A mid-ventral scent gland, located on the belly, serves to mark territory and communicate with other members of its species. The long vibrissae make it easy to navigate dark tunnels. By contentrating urine, the kidneys are able to conserve body water and prevent dehydration in times of water shortage.

The Djungarian hamster has twenty-eight chromosomes (fourteen pairs). It is naturally prone to the development of certain medical problems, especially cancer and obesity. Its reproduction is affected by daylight, temperature, water availability, and the presence or absence of the male hamster after breeding takes place. For these reasons, and because the Djungarian hamster is easy to breed and raise in captivity, it has been extensively studied for more than 50 years.

The Siberian Hamster, *Phodopus sungorus* (Winter White Russian Hamster)

History: Siberian hamsters are native to Kazakhstan, Manchuria, Mongolia, and Siberia. In 1968, four Siberian hamsters were trapped near Omsk in Siberia. These animals were used to establish a breeding colony at the Max-Planck Institute of Comparative Physiology in Germany. Eventually, animals from this colony were distributed to other research laboratories worldwide.

Description: The Siberian hamster is also called the Winter White Russian hamster because during the winter season most of its body coat color changes from gray to white. The hamster usually retains some gray coloration on its head and shoulders, and some small areas of gray on its body. This color change is influenced by changes in temperature and the photoperiod (the number of daylight hours to which the animal is exposed). In captivity, if conditions are right, the change in color from gray to white begins in mid-September and is complete by mid-November.

From February through March, the hamster's gray coloration begins to return. The black dorsal stripe, wider than that of the Djungarian hamster, extends all the way to the base of its tail. The dark ears are lined with white hairs. White fur extends from the belly and continues up the sides of the body. The white fur on the abdomen is separated from the gray coloration on the back by a thin line of brownish–black hairs. This area forms the "triple arch line." The muzzle, upper lip, lower cheeks, and tail are almost white.

The densely furred feet, responsible for the hamster's nickname, "striped hairy-footed hamster" are silvery white. They are a unique adaptation that helps maintain body warmth and makes it easier for the hamster to travel rapidly over sand dunes.

The Siberian hamster's face in profile is convex and its prominent eyes appear large and protruding. The body is stout and compact. Males measure approximately 4 inches (10 cm) from nose to rump. Females are slightly smaller at 3 inches (7.6 cm). Adults weigh between 1 and 2 ounces (28 to 56 g). Both sexes have a mid-ventral scent gland located on the abdomen. This gland is more developed in the male and is used for marking territory and communicating with other Siberian hamsters. Females have four pairs of mammary glands (eight teats).

Natural habitat and diet: The Siberian hamster is found in the steppes and grasslands of Manchuria, Mongolia, and Siberia. It digs tunnels 3 feet (1 m) deep leading to ground burrows where it can sleep, raise its family, and hide from predators (the weasel is one of the Siberian hamster's major enemies). Many burrows have four to six entrances. In the summer the burrows are lined with moss. To keep the burrow warm in the winter, the hamster closes all entrances except one and lines the burrow with animal fur or wool. The temperature inside the burrow is comfortable (62°F [16.7°C])

Chinese hamsters have more slender bodies and longer tails than Phodopus hamsters.

Dwarf Hamster Biology

	Djungarian Hamster *Phodopus campbelli*	Siberian Hamster *Phodopus sungorus*
Natural habitat	Steppes, dry steppes	Grasslands, steppes
Diet	Seeds	Seeds
Water source	Relies on insects	Vegetation, some insects
Number of chromosomes	28	28
Natural illness	Cancer, obesity	Diabetes
Ability to concentrate urine	Very efficient kidneys save body water	Efficient kidneys but less efficient than other *Phodopus*
Sensitivity to cold	Most sensitive of all *Phodopus*	Moderately sensitive
Sensitivity to heat	Very sensitive	Very sensitive

compared to the outside temperature ranges (–5°F to 72°F [–25°C to +23°C]).

The Siberian hamster eats the seeds of wild plants and grasses. It relies on plants in its diet to provide it with moisture. During times of drought, when vegetation is limited, it is able to survive on the moisture obtained from eating insects. Grasshoppers are a favorite.

Behavior: The Siberian hamster is good-natured and sociable, but group housing of adult males is not recommended. Studies have shown that even paired male housing is stressful, based on measuring cortisol (a hormone released during stress) levels in the animals. However, Siberian males can live together peacefully if they have been raised together since weaning, or if they are about the same age, and if they have enough space to hide from one another when tempers flare. They should also be about the same size, as larger

males will attempt to dominate and bully smaller males.

Compared to other dwarf hamsters, the Siberian hamster is slow and sluggish. Its behavior differs in many ways from that of its close relative, the Djungarian hamster. The Siberian hamster is less active in the evenings and spends less time scent-marking, and although the father Siberian hamster participates in raising the pups, he rarely is seen tending the pups alone in the nest. His role is not as crucial as that of the Djungarian hamster. Mother Siberian hamsters can raise their pups by themselves, if necessary.

Special characteristics: The Siberian hamster has cheek pouches for collecting and transporting food and bedding for hoarding. The hamster also uses its pouches as flotation devices by filling them with air when it is swimming. A mid-ventral scent gland on the

Desert Hamster *Phodopus roborovskii*	Chinese Hamster *Cricetulus griseus*
Deserts, semi-deserts	Steppes, semi-deserts
Seeds	Seeds
Less need for water than other *Phodopus*	Vegetation
34	22
No known predisposition	Diabetes
Most efficient kidney function of all *Phodopus*	Very efficient kidneys save body water
Least sensitive of all *Phodopus*	Moderately sensitive
Very sensitive	Very sensitive

abdomen, skin glands behind the ears, and glands in the corners of the cheek pouches serve to communicate social status, sex, and age to other members of the colony. The kidneys are specially adapted to conserve body water in a desert environment. The Siberian hamster is better adapted to cold temperatures than are many dwarf hamsters, and has been known to reproduce during the winter.

Siberian hamsters have developed an extraordinary energy saving adaptation, known as *torpor*. Torpor is a survival method that helps Siberian hamsters survive when temperatures drop, food is scarce, or day lengths shorten significantly. Torpor is not true hibernation, but it is a deep sleep in which the animal becomes sluggish and non-responsive to external stimuli. During torpor, a Siberian hamster's metabolism can drop 65 to 70 percent, its body temperature can fall from 99°F to 69°F (37°C to 21°C), and its heart rate can slow from a normal 349 beats per minute to 70 beats per minute.

Torpor is most affected by environmental temperature and can be induced when the ambient temperature drops to 41°F (5°C). Torpor can last several hours. During torpor a Siberian hamster's blood glucose (sugar) drops significantly.

Siberian hamsters born late in the breeding season when conditions are difficult (e.g., cold weather, food shortages) can conserve energy and cope temporarily with the demands of growth and survival by undergoing torpor immediately after weaning. It takes a while for a Siberian hamster to come out of torpor, at least forty minutes, and for the first four hours after the animal has come out of torpor its learning and recognition abilities are impaired.

The Siberian hamster has twenty-eight chromosomes (fourteen pairs). It has been the sub-

TIP

✔ All the dwarf hamsters are very sensitive to heat and cannot tolerate high temperatures.

✔ *P. campbelli* is more sensitive to cold and less able to adapt to cold than *P. sungorus.*

✔ *P. roborovskii* is better at concentrating urine and preserving body water than *P. campbelli.*

✔ *P. campbelli* is better at concentrating urine and preserving body water than *P. sungorus.*

ject of study for many years. Siberian hamsters may spontaneously develop diabetes mellitus. By studying *Phodopus sungorus*, scientists have gained important knowledge and information about this disease.

The Desert Hamster, *Phodopus roborovskii* (Roborovskii hamster)

History: The Desert hamster, *Phodopus roborovskii*, was named after the Roborovskii and Kozlov Russian expedition to Nan Shan. During this expedition in July 1894, a Desert hamster was captured and preserved.

Description: The Desert hamster is native to China, Mongolia, and Russia. It is the smallest of the *Phodopus* genus. Sizes of Desert hamsters vary, depending upon the region where they are found; however, on average, this small animal is only 2 inches (5.1 cm) in length. Its short, soft, fine-textured fur ranges in color from yellow–gold to sandy, to pink–beige, to gray. The undercoat is gray. Unlike *P. campbelli*

and *P. sungorus,* it lacks a dorsal stripe. The mouth area, limbs, belly, and tail are white. There is a large white patch above each eye and a small white patch at the base of each ear. The backs of the ears are gray or black at the top and white near the base. This coloration may be a defense mechanism, as it makes the hamster look as though it has eyes on the back of its head. The feet are short, broad, and covered with thick, white fur. The mid-ventral scent gland is larger in the male and used for marking territory and communicating with other members of its species. The female has four pairs of mammary glands (eight teats).

This good-natured animal is quick and active. Its small size and skill at escaping make it a challenge to handle and house. Desert hamsters are the least common of the dwarf hamsters usually found in pet stores.

Natural habitat: In the wild, the Desert hamster lives in sandy desert and semiarid areas where there is little vegetation. It digs steep burrows extending 2 to 6 feet (61 to 183 cm) into the ground. Researchers have found nest areas in these burrows lined with sheep wool and camel hair, and food storage areas full of seeds and insects.

Behavior: When it comes to temperament, the Desert hamster has received mixed reviews. Some people claim the animal cannot be tamed, even when handled daily from birth, but the hamster's advocates insist it is gentle and easy to tame. In truth, every animal is different. Some are easier to tame than others. Desert hamsters are high strung and very active. Their natural hyperactivity can seem like wild, untamed behavior.

The Desert hamster is a fast and jumpy animal. It can easily escape and is difficult to cap-

ture, the exact behavior that enables it to elude predators and to survive in the wild. Considering its tiny size and wild origin, the Desert hamster's ability to adapt to life in captivity and tolerate being handled is remarkable.

Fastidious cleanliness is the order of the day for the Desert hamster. It grooms itself numerous times daily and even interrupts its play to make sure every hair is in place. Part of its grooming routine includes dust baths (see Accommodations, page 45), which it enjoys immensely.

The Desert hamster is very active in the late evening, especially in November. It will live peacefully with other members of its species if they have been raised together from an early age. Like the other *Phodopus* hamsters, the male Desert hamster is an important part of the family unit and helps the mother raise their newborn pups.

Special characteristics: The Desert hamster has internal cheek pouches that can hold huge quantities of food and material. It has a mid-ventral scent gland on its belly, and kidneys capable of significant water conservation, allowing the animal better adaptation to its desert environment. Of the three dwarf hamster species, the Desert hamster has the most efficient kidney function with respect to its ability to concentrate urine and conserve water, so it is appropriately named.

The genetics of the Desert hamster have been studied extensively. The Desert hamster has thirty-four chromosomes (seventeen pairs). Certain features of the chromosomes indicate that the Desert hamster is more primitive than the other two members of its genus, *P. campbelli* and *P. sungorus*.

The Desert hamster has been reported to live longer than other members of the *Phodopus* genus, with a life span of two to three and a half years.

The Chinese Hamster

History: Scientific authorities report the first Chinese hamster was captured in Beijing (formerly Peking), China, and sold as a pet. At that time, the Chinese hamster population had reached an alarming size, and the animals plagued and destroyed agricultural regions. The first documented reports of Chinese hamsters being used in research laboratories began in 1919 at the Peking Union Medical College (*A New Laboratory Animal* by E. T. Hsieh). Chinese hamsters were later exported to research laboratories in other countries. They were used for early parasite studies of leishmaniasis (Black Fever). They were also used to study influenza and other diseases, including diabetes. Because of their wild nature and irregularities in their reproductive cycle, they initially proved difficult to raise in captivity. In 1948 ten males and ten females were exported from China to the United States and a colony was later established at Harvard Medical School. Since that time, many colonies of Chinese hamsters have been developed throughout the world. Chinese hamsters have been kept as pets since the 1970s.

Description: The Chinese hamster *(Cricetulus griseus)* is so different from the three previously described *Phodopus* species of hamsters that it belongs to a completely separate genus. There are twelve species of hamsters in the genus *Cricetulus,* but only *Cricetulus griseus* is kept as a pocket pet. The Chinese hamster is referred to as a "ratlike" hamster because of its physical characteristics. The blunt muzzle, robust yet slender body, short legs, and long tail are reminiscent of a rat. The internal cheek pouches are huge and capable of transporting amazing quantities of material. Chinese hamsters have both mid-ventral and flank scent glands that are used to mark territory. The Chinese hamster is also known as the "striped hamster," the "striped-back hamster," or the "gray hamster."

Chinese hamsters are gray, brown–gray, or grayish black in color. Their fur is very soft. The ears are gray, and a dark dorsal stripe extends from the top of the head to the tip of the tail. The belly is light gray to ivory. The eyes are black. Males measure 4 to 5 inches (10 to 12.7 cm) in length and weigh little more than 1 ounce (35 g). Females are about one tenth smaller and have four pairs of mammary glands (eight teats).

Natural habitat and diet: The Chinese hamster comes from northeastern China and inhabits dry, open country and desert borders. The Chinese hamster is a very good climber and uses its long tail for balance and support. It is a good digger and can dig tunnels more than 3 feet (1 m) deep. At the end of the tunnel it makes a burrow consisting of several chambers for storing food and nesting material. Some burrows may have more than one entrance tunnel, making it easier to escape predators.

Its diet consists mostly of seeds and young plant shoots, with a preference for peas, soybeans, and millet seeds.

Behavior: In its natural environment, the Chinese hamster is far less sociable than the *Phodopus* dwarf hamsters. In captivity, it can be quite belligerent and intolerant of other hamsters. A female will fight with another female in her territory, with some fights lasting up to twenty minutes. Pregnant females are the most aggressive, especially toward young males. Some females are so aggressive toward males during the breeding season that they kill them. Males also fight with each other, but not as much as the females do; in fact, when in the presence of battling females, the males tend to fight less. However, the presence of fighting males does not stop the aggressive behavior of the females.

During the spring and summer, the Chinese hamster is active during the day and night. As the cold weather approaches, it becomes more nocturnal in its behavior. Although it does not hibernate, it does sleep for longer periods during the winter.

The Chinese hamster is very territorial and uses scent glands located on its flanks to mark its nests and preferred areas. It does this by vigorously scratching the scent gland with its hind foot, then usually dragging the genital area on the ground. The dragging action spreads the scents from the flank gland and the genital area onto the territory or object being marked.

When it is angry or feels threatened, the Chinese hamster will throw itself on its back and display its large, impressive, and sharp incisors. It also will chatter and grind its teeth when agitated.

If you want to house Chinese hamsters together, be sure to introduce them at a very early age and watch them closely to be certain they will tolerate each other and not fight (see Understanding Your Dwarf Hamster, page 35). Otherwise, to avoid possible stress, injuries, and bite wounds, it is safest to house Chinese hamsters individually.

Special characteristics: The Chinese hamster has huge internal cheek pouches. It can fill its cheek pouches so full that its head seems to make up one third of its body size!

Sexually mature male Chinese hamsters have very large and obvious testicles, relative to the

size of their bodies and compared to *Phodopus* hamsters.

A sexually mature male Chinese hamster, with his pouches filled to capacity, gray color, longer tail, and larger testicles, can be a less appealing sight than a tiny round *Phodopus* hamster. This probably partially accounts for the fact that the Chinese hamster is not as popular as the other dwarf hamsters. Yet, Chinese hamsters are friendlier toward humans than the other dwarf hamster species and they are also less likely to bite.

Some Chinese hamsters may spontaneously develop diabetes, which can be a hereditary trait in hamsters. In addition, Chinese hamsters have only twenty-two chromosomes, the smallest number compared with other rodent species. The Chinese hamster is often used for research to study genetics, diabetes, viral and bacterial diseases, hormones, and cancer.

BEFORE YOU BUY

Dwarf hamster species differ in appearance, personality, housing requirements, and social needs. They require good care and nutrition to live a healthy, happy life. You have lots to consider and important decisions to make before you bring your hamster home!

Special Considerations

Just because dwarf hamsters are small doesn't mean there isn't a lot to consider before you add one to the family. These busy animals have a mind and an agenda of their own. They are fascinating to watch and fun to hold, but they are not a lap pet and will not tolerate excessive petting or cuddling. On the other hand, if you enjoy relaxing and watching beautiful, inquisitive animals at work and play, then hamsters are great entertainers.

Hamsters have minimal requirements to ensure their success as healthy happy pets in captivity. Responsible pet ownership always involves a certain amount of planning, commitment, time, and expense. Too often, people buy pets on the spur of the moment when an animal pulls at their heartstrings through the pet shop window. These impulse buyers have not done their homework to learn what they need to know about their pet and its needs before they buy. Sadly, many of the people who purchase pets under these conditions are later disappointed. Even worse, many of the animals become unwanted, or neglected.

Now that you have fallen in love with dwarf hamsters, you want to know whether one of these small animals will be compatible with your lifestyle before introducing one (or more!) into your home. The following considerations can help you decide.

Your Lifestyle

You are the first consideration. Who you are, how you live, and what you do are important factors in assessing how well a dwarf hamster will fit into your lifestyle. The addition of a new pet should be nothing less than a happy and positive experience for you.

It has been well documented that pet ownership has many benefits. People who own animals have been known to derive certain medical benefits from the close human-animal bond they form. People who own pets feel wanted, needed, and loved; after all, their animals depend on them for food and care, and give affection and companionship in return. Caressing or holding an animal has been shown to reduce blood pressure in some cases, and it has been suggested that people who own pets live longer.

But pet ownership is not always easy. In addition to time and financial commitments, there is the sadness that accompanies an illness, loss, or death of an animal friend. And some people (such as those with allergies to pet dander, or with compromised immune systems) simply cannot have pets, no matter how much they love them.

So consider yourself first. Are you ready for a dwarf hamster?

Cost

Contrary to what many people think, the greatest expense of pet ownership is not the purchase price of the animal. Actually, the purchase price is usually insignificant compared to the costs involved in time, housing, food, space, toys, and veterinary care.

The price of a dwarf hamster will vary with supply and demand, the species, the animal's age, and sometimes with the coat color and texture. For the most part, dwarf hamsters are very affordable. They are reasonably priced within the range of most rodent pocket pets available in pet stores today.

Time

Fortunately, dwarf hamsters are not demanding pets and do not require a great deal of time. The number of hamsters you own will determine how frequently their cage needs to be cleaned (see Accommodations, page 45). Most cages do not need to be cleaned more than once a week. Fresh water and food must be provided daily (see Feeding Your Dwarf Hamster, page 59). It takes only a few minutes a day to check your hamster's food and water for availability and cleanliness. During this time you should also check to be sure the animal is healthy and doing well. Simply observe your pet for normal appearance and behavior. Daily handling is especially important if you want your hamster to remain tame. Just a few minutes a day handling and talking to your hamster will make it a more enjoyable pet.

Essential Materials

Dwarf hamsters require a few basic essentials:
✔ Safe, comfortable, escape-proof housing of sufficient size to accommodate necessities and toys
✔ A secure lid or door that latches securely
✔ Traveling container for trips to the veterinarian and hamster shows
✔ Nutritious food
✔ Feeders and dishes
✔ Water bottle, stainless steel sipper tube, and fresh water available at all times
✔ Nest boxes and hiding places, and hide-aways
✔ Safe chew sticks and chew toys to keep teeth evenly worn and healthy
✔ Interesting toys, tubes, and tunnels

✔ Running wheel for exercise

✔ Dust baths

Your hamster needs plenty of exercise. This is easy to provide in the form of an exercise wheel, which is not only a toy, but a necessity. Hamsters have been known to run miles in an evening simply by working out on their wheels. Your hamster will also be appreciative of any other toys or activities you offer to make its life interesting. Favorite hamster playthings include dust baths to roll in; ladders; ramps and non-poisonous branches to climb; and tubes and tunnels.

Space

Although your dwarf hamster is small, it still requires a cage large enough to provide exercise and lots of hiding spaces. The more hamsters you house together, the greater the cage space they will require. Be aware that not all species of hamsters can be housed together.

Animals housed together must be:

✔ The same species. Do not house different species together; they will fight and can injure or kill one another.

✔ The same size. Bigger hamsters will dominate, bully, bite, and injure smaller hamsters.

✔ The same age. House hamsters together when they are very young so they can grow up amicably together. Do not introduce animals after they are twelve weeks of age or sexually mature.

✔ The same sex (unless you plan on having a hamster litter soon!).

Finding just the right location for your pet's cage is important. It must be out of direct sunlight, especially if the cage is made of glass or Plexiglas. Even if the temperature in your home is comfortable, a cage placed in direct sunlight can heat up rapidly, just like a greenhouse, and the inside of the cage can become extremely hot. Do not place your hamster's cage near any heat source, such as a fireplace, radiator, or furnace. Dwarf hamsters are very sensitive to the heat and can quickly die from heatstroke. It is also important to place the cage in an area away from cold and drafts. Although hamsters can tolerate the cold better than they can tolerate heat, if they are chilled they can develop pneumonia and die. This is especially true for baby hamsters.

The ideal temperature range for dwarf hamsters in captivity is between 69°F to 70°F (21°C to 22.2°C). Although dwarf hamsters can tolerate lower temperatures, they can suffer from heatstroke at higher temperatures. Ideal humidity for a dwarf hamster is 55 percent. Dwarf hamsters are physiologically well adapted to the arid conditions of their ancestor's origins, but they should not be subjected to humidity levels below 40 percent or they can suffer from skin and other health problems.

Finally, place your hamster's housing at a comfortable level for viewing and handling. A location where you can enjoy your pet's activities and be able to feed it, clean the cage, change the water bottle, and replace the bedding without having to bend or stoop is ideal.

Other Household Pets

One of the biggest threats to a dwarf hamster is the presence of another animal. Hamsters have a keen sense of smell. They know when there are other animals in the house. Your hamster will become stressed or frightened if your other pets come near its cage. Make sure the lid to your hamster's cage is securely fastened. Be sure to place the cage well out of reach of the family dog, cat, ferret, bird, or any other pet. You probably never thought of your house pets as being harmful, but cats and ferrets are natural hunters and dogs can play rough—and pet reptiles would find your hamster just the right size to eat. Even small birds can quickly peck a small rodent to death, so be sure not to leave your hamster unattended in its cage inside or on a porch where pets or wild birds can find it. Although hamsters can behave ferociously when frightened and inflict serious bite wounds, they are no match for these animals. For the safety of all the pets in your household, keep your hamster isolated.

Children

Inquisitive small children are naturally drawn to animals and interesting containers. For everyone's viewing enjoyment, place your hamster's cage where its activities can be easily observed. Small children should be supervised at all times when watching or handling the hamster. It is

Ideally, your veterinarian will have a special interest and expertise in hamster health care.

safest if children sit down and hold the hamster with both hands so that there is less chance of dropping a squirming animal. Some children are too young to learn that they may handle an animal only when in the presence of adults. In this situation, the safety of the young child and the hamster is your responsibility. When you cannot be there to supervise their activity, place the hamster cage out of the reach of children. This is a safety measure well worth the temporary inconvenience.

Nocturnal Activities

Hamsters are very busy during the night. If you do not share your pet's nocturnal schedule, you will want to find a place in your home where its nighttime activities, such as digging and running in the exercise wheel, do not keep you awake.

Veterinary Care

Hamsters are generally hardy animals that do very well with good care and nutrition; however, if your pet becomes sick or injured, you will need to take it to your veterinarian for an examination and possible treatment. If you own several hamsters and one of them is sick, it is important to determine the cause of illness and ensure that the problem is not contagious to your other pets.

Many veterinarians specialize in pocket pets, or have a special interest in these very small animals. Pocket pets have nutritional, housing, and medical requirements that are very different from those of the larger companion animals. They also are sensitive to certain products and medications used for treating other pets.

It is a good idea to contact veterinarians in advance of needing veterinary care. This gives you an opportunity to introduce yourself and meet the veterinarians. You can then decide beforehand where you would like to take your hamster if it becomes ill, and not be burdened with this decision during an emergency.

When to Acquire a New Pet

Although you may want a dwarf hamster right now, today might not be the best time to buy your pet. Hamster breeders or pet shops may not have available exactly what you have in mind. You may need to place a special order to reserve just the right hamster. Be sure to take the time you need to buy exactly what you want. It's worth the wait and you won't be disappointed.

If you have several obligations and your free time is limited, postpone buying a new pet until you have more time to enjoy it. For example, if you are moving or changing jobs, a new pet may add stress rather than enjoyment. If you are planning a vacation soon, you will have to make arrangements for animal care while you are gone.

Hamsters, like many pets, are often purchased during the holidays as gifts. This brings up some very important points:

✔ Although it is tempting, it is never a good idea to buy a pet as a gift. Pet ownership is a responsibility that someone else may not want to assume.

✔ Adding a new pet to the family during the holiday season should be discouraged. This is a time when most people are busy with visitors. Holidays are usually noisy and bright. Dwarf hamsters have keen, sensitive hearing and are startled by loud sounds and bright lights. A new pet can be overlooked in the shuffle with all the distractions and excitement, and families do not have time to learn about, observe, socialize, and care for a new pet during the holidays.

✔ Visitors and guests unfamiliar with proper handling techniques may stress and frighten the new hamster or unintentionally hurt it. They may also be bitten.

✔ Someone may forget to close the cage door or lid. Holidays are a time when many pets escape from home, and hamsters are good escape artists.

✔ Pets bought during the holidays may be more stressed or prone to illness than usual. With the greater demand for pets during this time, animals may be separated from their mothers and weaned too early, or shipped long distances. These stressful situations can lead to illness and even death. There are, of course, animal protection laws, but it is good to be aware of potential problems.

What to Consider

Dwarf hamsters may be purchased from hamster breeders and hobbyists, individuals advertising in a newspaper, and local pet stores. Hamster breeders may be contacted through clubs and organizations, local veterinarians, advertisements in specialty pet magazines, or the Internet.

Whenever possible, look at as many hamsters as you can before you make a selection so that you can compare the overall health and quality of the animals, the cleanliness of their environment, and the different price ranges.

Once you have selected a hamster to take home, ask if you can pick it up and hold it before you buy it. You will quickly learn how tame the hamster is by how well it behaves when you handle it. If it tries to attack or bite, continue your search for a friendlier individual.

You may be thinking about raising dwarf hamsters as a hobby. In this case, contact the hamster club nearest you for a list of reputable hamster breeders. An experienced hamster breeder can be a valuable source of information and answer many questions about available animals, color varieties, and hamster shows.

Hamster clubs are a lot of fun. Members share information ranging from health tips to required standards for hamster exhibition. Clubs are a good way to meet other people who share your interests in these fascinating creatures.

Which Species to Select

There are four species of dwarf hamsters from which to choose. Each species has its own unique physical appearance, personality, and behavioral characteristics. Hamsters also differ in their housing requirements. Very small hamsters, such as the Desert hamster, *P. roborovskii,* are difficult to house in wire cages. Some hamsters, such as the *Phodopus* hamsters, can live together peacefully all the time, or at certain times in their breeding cycle. On the other hand, Chinese hamsters, *C. griseus,* will often fight viciously with one another and prefer to live alone.

The hamster you select will depend on your personal preferences:
✔ Which animal appeals most to you?
✔ Will you be breeding your hamster?
✔ Which species do you find most attractive?
✔ Which are the most playful and interesting to you?
✔ Which one would be the best match for you and your lifestyle, considering the amount of housing space you can provide and the number of animals you wish to buy?

Make sure the hamster you choose is healthy. Check to be sure:
✔ the eyes are clear and bright
✔ the coat is well groomed
✔ there is no discharge from the eyes, ears, or nose
✔ there are no signs of diarrhea, constipation, or dehydration

Which Hamster to Choose?

Djungarian hamster	Siberian hamster	Desert hamster	Chinese hamster
Campbell's	Winter White	Roborovskii	*Cricetulus griseus*
Phodopus campbelli	*Phodopus sungorus*	*Phodopus roborovskii*	
Most readily available	Readily available	Less readily available	Least available
Most color varieties	Limited colors	One basic color	Two basic colors
Most likely to bite	Easy to handle, easy to tame, friendly	Quick and difficult to handle	Easy to handle, friendly

✔ the hamster is compact, and not thin
✔ the hamster is young
✔ the teeth are properly aligned
✔ the hamster is inquisitive and active

How Many Dwarf Hamsters to Keep

How many dwarf hamsters you wish to keep will be up to you, based on your plans for your pet. A hamster makes a wonderful companion and can serve as an excellent educational tool for children and adults. Hamsters are fun to exhibit at shows. They help create new friend-ships by bringing together people who share the same interests. Keeping hamsters can become a full-time hobby. If you decide to raise and exhibit hamsters, you will find yourself studying their ancestry, genetics, and inheritance of coat color and texture. The number of hamsters you own will depend upon your interests, hamster stock availability, the amount of housing space you can provide, your hamster's compatibility with other hamsters, and the amount of time and money you wish to invest.

Hamsters should be fun. You never want to own so many animals that it seems you spend more time cleaning up after them than enjoying them. Keep your animal numbers reasonable so most of the time you spend with your hamsters will be fun time.

Male or Female?

The decision to acquire a male or a female hamster will depend on your reasons for buying a hamster. If you are simply looking for a good pet and an interesting companion, you will be happy with either a male or female hamster. If you are planning to raise hamsters, you will need at least one pair to begin your project.

The main physical difference you will note is that the male hamster is slightly larger than the female, his scrotum is visible when viewed from the rear and the mid-ventral scent gland on the abdomen is more apparent. The main behavioral difference is the male's tendency to scent-mark his territory more frequently (see Understanding Your Dwarf Hamster, page 35). Don't worry. Although your hamster's scent can be detected by other animals, to you it will be virtually odorless.

Because some hamsters can be housed together and some cannot, your choice of a male or female will also depend on the species of hamster you have selected and the total number of hamsters you will be housing.

Species Compatibility

	Male/ Female pairs	Male/ Male pairs	Female/ Female pairs	Group housing	Safe to house with different species?
Djungarian/ Campbell's	Yes	No	Yes	Yes	No
Siberian/ Winter White	Yes	Sometimes, but not advised; use caution	Yes, but may quarrel	Yes	No
Desert/ Roborovskii	Yes	Yes, but prefers colonial group housing	Yes, but prefers colonial group housing	Yes	No
Chinese	Females can be very aggressive toward males and kill them	Yes, but use caution; most Chinese hamsters prefer solitary housing	No	Use caution; make sure animals do not fight	No

Age and Longevity

The ideal age to bring your new hamster home is when it is recently weaned and no longer needs its mother for nutrition, warmth, and survival. There are two good reasons to buy a young hamster rather than an older one: First, a baby hamster is gentler and easier to handle and tame; it will adapt quickly to you and its new home. Second, dwarf hamsters have short life spans; the sooner you acquire your hamster, the more time you will have to enjoy it.

How long do dwarf hamsters live? The life span will vary with each animal and the care and nutrition it receives. On average, the Djungarian hamster, *Phodopus campbelli,* and the Siberian hamster, *Phodopus sungorus,* live one and one half to two years. The Chinese hamster,

Cricetelus griseus, may live up to three years. The Desert hamster, *Phodopus roborovskii,* has the longest life span, approximately three and one half years.

During this short time you will develop a strong emotional attachment to your endearing pet and when it dies you will experience the heartache that accompanies such a loss. On the positive side, hamster ownership does not impose a long-term commitment, as with a dog that may live to be sixteen, or a parrot that can live fifty years!

If you already know you want hamsters to be part of your life for several years, keep two or more hamsters at a time. Having more than one hamster will help ease the sorrow and fill the void when a hamster dies.

Children and Dwarf Hamsters

Dwarf hamsters make interesting and educational pets for children. They must learn however, that most hamsters prefer to be watched rather than held or petted.

With adult guidance, children can learn a lot from a pet hamster including the importance of humane care and treatment and respect for life. Children can learn about the hamster's activities, play behavior, favorite foods, and even its reproduction—it is fascinating to see how a little creature can be such a good parent while it raises a family.

A hamster in the house is a great way for very young children to learn to be responsible. They can participate in the hamster's care and learn about the importance of fresh water, good food, and a clean home for their pet. Older children can learn about animal behavior, color genetics, and hamster reproduction.

Adult supervision is always necessary when a child is handling a hamster in order to prevent accidental bite injuries to the child, and accidental injury to the hamster or escape if it is dropped.

A hamster can open doors of communication and learning for a child. Together, you and a child can share thoughts and ideas about animals, people, families, and anything else you can relate to hamsters and humans on the child's level.

Animal Life and Death

Even with the best possible care, hamsters eventually become ill or die. Dwarf hamsters have a relatively short life span. They do not demand a long-term commitment from you or your child. This is an advantage if your child's hobbies change over time and interest in the

hamster dwindles. On the other hand, if your child still enjoys having a hamster in the house, and the hamster is aging, now is an excellent time to buy another hamster.

Children are very sensitive to issues of animal life and death. The death of a pet hamster may be the first loss a child experiences. It is very important that the child be prepared in advance for the eventual, and inevitable, loss or death of a beloved pet and that this preparation be provided in a compassionate manner appropriate for the child's age and level of maturity. The loss of a pet can be a very emotional experience for a child, but if handled skillfully, this loss can be turned into a positive learning experience. It provides an opportunity in which you may openly discuss life, love, illness, or death and possibly address additional fears or concerns the child may have. A small hamster can play a big part in helping a child grow, mature, and strengthen in character.

UNDERSTANDING YOUR DWARF HAMSTER

Dwarf hamsters are complicated creatures. They communicate through body language, scent, sound, and touch. Many of their complex behaviors are instinctive; others are learned. The more you understand your hamster and its unique personality, the more you will enjoy it!

Hamsters have an undeserved reputation for being aggressive, ill-tempered, and quick to bite; however, this behavior usually follows a sudden disturbance or mishandling. Often, hamsters only threaten to bite. With some practice and a little patience, most dwarf hamsters can be tamed and fun to hold. Of course, you will want to interact with your hamster under ideal circumstances so select a time when you are not in a hurry, preferably in the evening when your hamster is in a playful, happy mood. It is easy to know if the time is right and your hamster is feeling sociable. Hamsters communicate in many ways, and they are quick to make their feelings known, especially if they are feeling irritable. Here are some basic dwarf hamster behaviors to help you learn how to interpret your hamster's body language and voice signals.

The Basics

Body Language

Dwarf hamsters are very expressive. You will easily recognize the times your hamster feels comfortable and secure. Its sense of well-being is obvious as it runs about its cage, busily digging, climbing, grooming, and exploring. Sometimes your hamster will feel so playful it will even leap or flip in the air. These gymnastics are all signs of a happy, healthy hamster.

Curiosity and interest: When your hamster is curious or interested in something, it will sit up on its haunches and sniff the air for long periods of time. Its position will be relaxed, with its front legs held about level with its belly and its front toes pointing toward the ground.

Fear: If your pet is startled or frightened, it may become aggressive and threatening. It will tilt its ears back and stand with one or both front feet raised. It may hiss or squeak, or grind its teeth. This stance is not a bluff—your hamster is upset and agitated and considering an attack. It is ready to bite. Let your hamster calm down for a while before you attempt to pick it up or remove it from its cage, or you may be bitten.

A frightened hamster may assume a defensive posture. It will throw itself backwards, lie on its back, and expose its vulnerable underside—but this doesn't mean it will not bite. The hamster will continue to threaten by displaying its large incisors, which it will use if necessary. There is no doubt a hamster in this position can be dangerous.

Emotions and intentions: Hamsters use body language as one way to let other hamsters know their emotions and intentions. A young male who is afraid of an older, larger, or more powerful male will raise his tail and walk stiffly. He may squeal. Clearly he is indicating he would rather be somewhere else than in such a precarious situation. A male hamster that is being attacked by a female will raise both front paws in defense. Female hamsters are seldom hurt by the males, yet some females will kill male hamsters. The male will use his front paws to rebuff an aggressive female if there is nowhere for him to run and hide.

Yawning is another way a hamster shows it feels threatened, is angry, stressed, or in an aggressive mood. Of course, yawning may just mean your pet is sleepy or bored. You must consider the circumstances to correctly interpret your pet's body language.

Grooming: Grooming is an excellent sign that your hamster is comfortable and feels at ease.

Breeding: During the breeding period, body language is one of the many important ways hamsters communicate that the time is right for mating (see Raising Dwarf Hamsters, page 79). The male hamster will sniff the female's head and ears and then examine under her tail. If the female is receptive, she will hold her back flat and firm, brace her legs, and raise her tail. If the female is not ready to breed, she will bite the male on his face and scrotum.

It is important that hamsters housed together always have a way to escape each other's temper tantrums. Several hiding places and a lot of space are necessary when more than one hamster shares a cage.

Unfamiliar territory: Hamsters have poor eyesight and rely on their vibrissae and sense of smell to find a safe path. You will notice that your hamster will flatten itself out and slink about when you set it in unfamiliar territory. Because your hamster is unsure of its way, it looks as if it is clutching the earth and trying not to fall. Without its own scent marks to guide it, your hamster will feel uneasy in new surroundings.

A frightened hamster may become aggressive and bite.

Sleeping: Hamsters spend a lot of time sleeping. You may not find your hamster right away if it is sleeping, because hamsters like to bury themselves in bedding material and hide while they snooze. Sometimes a hamster can be in such a deep sleep that you might worry it is dead until you watch closely for its almost imperceptible breathing. Remember that a dozing hamster can be easily startled and wake up in an irritable mood. If your hamster is asleep, make sure it hears you and has sufficient time to awaken. Allow your pet time to stretch and yawn and sniff the air, then approach slowly and handle it gently.

Your hamster has specific inherited behaviors characteristic to its species. Other aspects of its personality will depend on the positive experiences you provide. Your pet will be easy to tame and more enjoyable because you recognize and respect its body language.

Vocalizations

Hamsters do not make many sounds and they save their talk for important situations. For example, if a hamster is frightened, it may squeak loudly. When a hamster is threatening to attack, it will chatter, grind its teeth, or squeak. Usually, teeth chattering is a more serious threat and more aggressive behavior than squeaking. A hamster may also make sounds similar to a hiss or growl. Male hamsters sometimes hiss and growl immediately after breeding.

Some of the sounds a hamster makes are in the ultrasonic range, beyond human hearing. Baby and adult hamsters can call to one another without being heard by some predators. This is a remarkable adaptation for survival in the wild.

Scent-marking

Scent-marking is an important hamster activity. Hamsters scent-mark their territory by rubbing their scent glands against surfaces. Scent glands secrete a chemical substance containing pheromones, chemical signals that can be perceived by other animals. Hamsters use their keen sense of smell to identify their nests and each other, and to determine when the time is right for breeding.

Phodopus hamsters have mid-ventral scent glands; Chinese hamsters have both mid-ventral and flank scent glands. Small scent glands are also located around the hamster's genital area.

Activity

Dwarf hamsters are most active during the evening, but they have short periods of activity during the day. Activity level is seasonal and decreases as the days grow shorter and the temperature drops. At temperatures of 40°F to 60°F (4.4°C to 16°C), some dwarf hamsters will enter a deep sleep, called a torpor. This is not a true state of hibernation, although some of the

A dwarf hamster can run more than a mile each night in its wheel!

animal's body systems, including heart rate and breathing, slow to the point that normal handling may fail to arouse it. This condition may last for several days in cold weather. Since most homes are kept warm during the winter, you may not observe this behavior in your hamster. If you do, don't mistake it for illness or death—and be careful not to waken your hamster in this condition or it may bite!

Hamsters are great escape artists, and most escape efforts take place at night. Be sure to close and secure the cage before bedtime, and make sure there are no openings to squeeze through and no way to chew out. Unlike rats and gerbils, hamsters will not return to their cages after escaping. If your pet escapes, you may have to set humane traps to capture it. If you cannot purchase a humane trap, a ramp leading into a baited bucket set up against the wall may work as a safe and suitable trap.

Hoarding

Dwarf hamsters have well-developed cheek pouches that make it possible for them to collect and transport large quantities of food.

Recent studies show that when Siberian hamsters are fasted (food withheld), their bodies can release a specific chemical (Agouti-related protein or AgRP). This chemical can stimulate Siberian hamsters to hoard up to ten times more food than they normally would. Interestingly, the chemical triggers the search for food, but once they find food, the hamsters hoard most of it, rather than eat it. Other studies show that female Siberian hamsters increased hoarding and food intake during pregnancy and lactation.

The instinct to hoard food for future use is very strong; as a result, hamsters gather huge quantities of food and stockpile it in various locations throughout the cage. Your pet will hoard more food than it will ever need. Hoarded food should be removed when the cage is cleaned to prevent spoilage, contamination, and overfeeding.

Hiding

Hamsters love to hide; after all, they are naturally burrow-dwelling animals. They love to tunnel under things and cover themselves with shavings or bedding material. Your hamster is following two protective instincts by hiding while it sleeps: It is keeping warm, and it is hiding from predators. Your pet will enjoy having several hiding places; they make the cage interesting for it and also make it feel secure.

So, if you cannot find your hamster right away, do not panic. Gently move some bedding material around and look under some objects. Your pet is sure to be in there somewhere.

Play Behavior

When hamsters play, their happiness is contagious. They run, jump, leap, and flip. They investigate every nook and cranny, explore every toy, and climb every ladder—no wonder they sleep so much! A healthy hamster is very active during its playtime.

Social Behavior

Each species of dwarf hamster has different social behaviors. Some can live together peacefully in small colonies; others prefer to live alone. Most dwarf hamsters will be compatible if they are not stressed or overcrowded. In fact, some dwarf hamsters form monogamous pairs and raise families together (see Raising Dwarf Hamsters, page 79).

What to consider as you decide how to group your hamsters:

1. Differences in temperament vary depending on the species and the unique personality of each hamster.

2. Usually, if hamsters are housed together by sex (males housed with males; females housed with females) at the time of weaning, or before they reach sexual maturity, they will accept each other. This type of group housing requires enough space that the animals will not be stressed or agitated from overcrowding.

3. Hamsters need secure hiding areas within their cage where they can find privacy or escape from a fight.

4. Unless you are planning on raising hamsters, males and females should be separated before they reach sexual maturity. If adult hamsters of the same sex insist on fighting with each other, they should be housed individually.

5. Encounters between adult Djungarian males often result in death of one of the males. *Adult males of this species should always be housed separately.*

6. Encounters between adult Siberian males cause a display of aggression. Eventually, a dominance hierarchy, or "pecking order," is established. The males may eventually live together peacefully but fights break out again if a new male joins the group. It is best not to house adult males together.

7. A mature female hamster will fight with a male if he tries to breed when she is not receptive. She may even kill him.

8. A female hamster may fight with other females and males if she is trying to protect a litter.

9. A male hamster will fight with other males, but will rarely attempt to harm a female.

10. Hamsters of one species will fight with hamsters of a different species.

11. Hamsters will also fight with other species of rodents.

12. Hamsters compete intensely for toys, especially for use of the running wheel. Be sure there are enough playthings for all. If you can, give your hamsters an additional running wheel to avoid quarreling.

Preventing Social Problems

If you decide to house your pets together, make sure they are compatible. A good understanding of species behavior and individual personalities is essential.

Be prepared to prevent fights. Test your hamsters for compatibility. Ways to introduce new hamsters and test for compatibility:

✔ Introduce the new hamster into the cage with the others, but keep them separated by a

wire mesh screen or Plexiglas divider so they can see and smell each other, but not fight.

✔ Take the shavings or bedding material from the new hamster's cage and mix it with bedding from the established hamsters' cage, combining their scents. Next, place the hamsters together and make sure they do not fight.

✔ Thoroughly clean a cage and add fresh shavings or bedding material. Place the new hamster in the cage and then add the established hamsters a few moments later.

✔ If the hamsters enjoy dust baths, give them the same dust baths to use, then put them together in a clean cage containing new shavings or bedding material.

✔ The animals can be distracted from fighting with each other by adding food treats and interesting new toys to the cage.

✔ Always observe the animals closely and if they start to fight, separate them and try again later.

Not all hamsters will live together in harmony or share parental obligations. For the safety and well-being of your hamsters, separate or group them according to their species-specific behavior. Always keep a cage separator or additional cages on hand in case there is a sudden problem. If you are uncertain how your hamsters will treat each other, then house them individually until you can test them for compatibility.

Aggressive Behavior

When a dwarf hamster behaves aggressively, there's usually a good reason. In addition to sudden disturbances, mishandling, and inappropriate housing conditions, pregnancy is a major cause of aggressive behavior.

Pregnant hamsters are usually very aggressive. For your safety, and the safety of the future litter, mothers-to-be should be disturbed as little as possible during the gestation (pregnancy) period.

Mother hamsters will also behave aggressively toward you. If you reach in the cage while there is a litter, you run the risk of being bitten. Mother hamsters often misdirect their aggression toward their young; it is not uncommon for a mother hamster to eat, or cannibalize, her babies. This cannibalistic behavior occurs more frequently with first-time mothers, but can happen with any mother hamster.

Female hamsters tend to fight with each other more than male hamsters. A female hamster that does not want to breed can be particularly aggressive toward an inquiring male hamster. The female will bite the male on the head and body, and especially on his scrotum. In the wild, the male can run and hide, but in a closed cage the male has nowhere to go. Remove him immediately.

Repetitive Behavior

Repetitive behavior, such as constant bar chewing, circling, jumping up and down in one place, pacing, and nonstop fur chewing, are behavioral problems that indicate your hamster is bored, stressed, upset, or agitated. Behavioral problems can be prevented by making your pet's cage interesting and giving plenty of toys to chew and lots of things to explore. Once a repetitive behavior has been established, it is difficult, if not impossible, to stop.

HOW-TO: HANDLING

There are several ways you can pick up your dwarf hamster without harm to either one of you.

To avoid being bitten, before you pick up your dwarf hamster, make sure that it is not sleeping. Don't wake your pet up suddenly and don't make any sudden movements or noises that could frighten it.

The Can, Jar, or Tube Technique

This method is a good one for children who are learning to handle a dwarf hamster for the first time. Slowly lower a can, jar, or small PVC tube (a toilet paper tube or paper towel tube will also work) into the cage and place it in front of the animal so that it is facing the inside of the container. Hamsters are naturally curious and like to crawl into small spaces, so your hamster may

decide to crawl in without any prodding. If you are using a clear jar, it is easy to watch your pet while you catch it. If your hamster needs some encouragement, hold the jar in one hand and use your other hand to gently push its rump forward so it enters the jar. Be sure to keep the top of the can or jar covered (or, if using a tube, be sure *both* ends are covered) because your hamster may try to jump out while you are transporting it.

The Two-Handed Technique

This method is an excellent technique to use on gentle, tame hamsters. Place both hands together to form a cup and slowly lower your hands into the cage. Use your hands like a scoop to slide underneath the animal and lift it out of the cage. You may prefer to slide one hand under

your pet and cup your other hand over the top of it. Be sure to keep your hands cupped tightly so your hamster doesn't find a small hole to wiggle out of and fall.

The One-Handed Technique

This technique allows you to lift the hamster out of the cage without exposing fingertips to a possible bite. Slowly lower one hand into the cage above the hamster's back, with the fingers directed toward the animal's rump. Grasp the pet around its middle with your thumb, little finger, and ring finger. The middle and index fingers support the hamster by the rump, while the palm of the hand rests on the back of its head, allowing a firm hold while lifting the animal gently from its cage. A dwarf hamster that feels secure will seldom attempt to bite or struggle to free itself; however, because dwarf hamsters are so small, this technique works best for adult hamsters, and may be difficult or awkward for someone with large hands.

Scruff-of-the-Neck Technique

Many people cringe at the thought of lifting an animal by the skin on the back of its

Gently scoop up your hamster, using a jar or a can.

Use both hands to pick up your hamster.

neck, but this technique is very safe and humane for hamsters, when done gently. The hamster has large cheek pouches, so there is a lot of loose skin around its neck and down its back. Approach your hamster calmly and let it know you are there. This way your hamster will not be startled and should not roll on its back and threaten to bite. Slowly lower your hand into the cage and place your hand flat on your hamster's back. It will naturally try to flatten itself against the floor of the cage and may continue to slink about in this flattened position. With your hand flat over your pet's back, grasp the skin on either side of its neck and back between your thumb and fingers. There are some disadvantages to this method: First, you need to keep a good grasp on the hamster's skin because it can turn around in its skin and bite you; second, the hamster's eyes may appear to protrude and this can be startling. Your pet's eyes will return to normal appearance as soon as you release it. Finally, your hamster may let any food that may be stored in its cheek pouches empty out suddenly. This may look as if your pet is vomiting or in pain, but it is not.

Walk-onto-the-Wire-Mesh Technique

If you have a small piece of screen, or wire mesh, you can encourage your pet to climb on the mesh platform and cling to it until you can transfer your pet into a new cage. Place a special treat on the wire mesh and your hamster might climb right on board. Gently cover your hamster with the palm of your hand while you transfer it, so that it doesn't jump or fall off the mesh platform.

Glove Technique

Some people prefer to use thick gloves when handling hamsters for the first time. This is unnecessary and cumbersome and sometimes gives a person a false sense of security, because a hamster can still bite through thick gloves. Because it is difficult to restrain a small animal with thick gloves, there is a tendency to hold on too tightly, squeezing the hamster and making it hard for it to breathe, without even knowing you are harming it.

Warning: *Forceps, tweezers, or other instruments should never be used to grasp hamsters.*

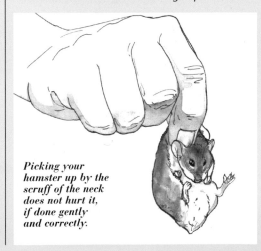

Picking your hamster up by the scruff of the neck does not hurt it, if done gently and correctly.

ACCOMMODATIONS

Dwarf hamsters are hardy, resilient, resourceful rodents. Your pet's survival instincts are evident in its everyday activities and should be taken into consideration as you prepare its new home.

In their native habitats, dwarf hamsters are subjected to climatic changes that have placed exceptional demands on their ability to survive. Much of a hamster's survival in the wild depends on its ability to find just the right place to dig tunnels and build dens that are warm and out of the reach of predators. A hamster has to be creative and resourceful. It needs to find soft, warm bedding material and hoard plenty of food to help it through tough times.

Some dedicated hamster enthusiasts create large displays similar to those seen in zoological gardens. They fill them with sand, soil, and plants so the animals can be observed digging deep tunnels and building dens. However, most of us prefer to house our hamsters in a simple manner that is convenient and fits comfortably in a room of the house. Fortunately for us, dwarf hamsters are easy to please. We don't have to recreate miniature versions of the Russian steppes or the deserts of China for them to adapt to life in captivity. They are perfectly happy in almost any of the glass or Plexiglas tanks, or wire cages, available from pet stores.

Housing Considerations

One of the most important things to remember when deciding how to house your pet is that hamsters are rodents and rodents love to chew. They can chew their way out of any type of wooden confinement, and, because they are tiny, they can easily squeeze their way between the bars of some cages. Wooden cages or cages with widely spaced bars are not suitable for these excellent escape artists.

As desert rodents, hamsters have the remarkable ability to conserve body water and make better use of the limited water supply in the wild. One way hamsters do this is by concentrating their urine. Hamsters produce less urine than do some other rodent species, because there is less water content in hamster urine. Normal hamster urine has a cloudy, milky, thick appearance and an odor. Hamsters also preserve body water by resorbing fluid from the body waste materials as they pass through the intestines. Hamster feces are relatively dry compared to the droppings of other rodents, such as mice and rats. Since hamsters produce

Type of Housing

There are countless cage styles available in pet stores.

Housing/Cage Style	Advantage	Disadvantage
Aquarium	• Big enough to house four adult dwarf hamsters • Easy to observe animals • Protects animals from drafts and muffles noises • Nonporous • No litter scatter	• Poor ventilation • Heavy and difficult to clean
Wire cages	• Well ventilated • Can have tiers for more play space • Easy to clean and disinfect • Door can be at top or side of cage	• Wire bars may allow escape if too widely spaced • Wire-tiered levels are hard on small, delicate feet • Hamsters may fall from levels
Plastic cages	• Easy to see hamsters • Easy to clean	• Hamsters can chew plastic • Poor ventilation • Too small • Expensive • Not durable
Wooden cages	• Easy to build homemade cage any size	• Difficult to disinfect • Porous

small amounts of urine and very dry droppings, a cage housing four dwarf hamsters usually does not have to be cleaned more than once each week.

Housing Size

Dwarf hamsters are tiny, but your pets need as big a cage as you can possibly provide them. A large cage gives your hamsters space to explore. It also helps prevent overcrowding, stress, and repetitive behaviors. A large cage makes it easy for you to watch your hamsters.

Unless you buy a large cage, by the time you add all the cage accessories (e.g., running wheel, dishes, dust bath, hideaways, and toys), there will be very little room left for your pets to play.

At a minimum, floor space for two dwarf hamsters should be no less than 16 inches by 20 inches (40 cm by 50 cm). Height should be at least 16 inches (40 cm). A secure door or wire mesh top is necessary to prevent the hamsters from climbing or jumping out.

The cage size you select will depend upon the number of animals you are grouping together.

Make Sure

- Aquarium should not be placed near heat source

- Bars should be horizontal, not vertical
- Bar spacing should be 0.275 inch (7 mm) or less to prevent injury

- Hamster does not chew and choke on plastic particles

- Do not use cedar or pine
- Wood should not be chemically treated

A standard 10-gallon (38-L) tank can easily house two adult hamsters. To avoid overcrowding, do not keep more than four adult dwarf hamsters in a cage. When hamsters are stressed, they fight, and all breeding activities come to a halt. Female hamsters signal each other, through pheromones, when they are overcrowded. These signals cause a change in hormone levels and the females stop mating. If you want your hamsters to reproduce, you must make sure they have enough space in which to run around, hide, and play without being cramped.

Lighting (Photoperiod)

Your hamster's activities and breeding behavior are seasonal and are influenced by exposure to light. The hours of light exposure during the day is called the *photoperiod*. Each species of dwarf hamster responds differently to the long days of summer or the dark winter hours. For example, the Desert hamster, *P. roborovskii*, and the Siberian hamster, *P. sungorus,* are more active in November and less active in February and March. The Djungarian hamster, *P. campbelli*, is more active in February and less active in November.

The photoperiod is one of the most important influences in a dwarf hamster's life. Together with temperature, the photoperiod determines when a hamster is active, when it eats, when it sleeps, and when it breeds. Hamsters are so sensitive to the amount of light they receive that their metabolism, many of their various hormones, and their sexual development are affected by increased or decreased exposure to light. The correct amount of light exposure is a critical factor in successfully rearing dwarf hamsters.

For example, the onset of puberty (sexual maturity) in the Siberian hamster is determined by the photoperiod (see Raising Dwarf Hamsters, page 79). If the photoperiod is sixteen hours each day, then the baby males become sexually mature by thirty-five days of age. If the photoperiod is shortened to eight hours each day, the baby

males require 130 days to reach sexual maturity. The situation is similar for ovarian development in the baby female hamsters because of a decrease in the production of certain hormones. In the adult male hamster, an 8-hour photoperiod causes a 90 percent reduction in the size of the testicles.

The Siberian hamster's coat color is also affected by the photoperiod. When exposure to light is eight to ten hours each day, the coat color begins to change from gray to white. Remember, this color change is why many hamster fanciers call the Siberian hamster the Winter White hamster.

Hamsters do not like bright lights. Be sure to always give your hamster houses and hideaways where it can escape bright lighting and rest its eyes.

Reverse-Light Cycle

If you would like your hamsters to be active during the day, it is possible to do this by changing their light cycle to what is called a "reverse-light cycle." This means that during the evening hours they are in a well-lighted or daylight-filled room, so they sleep most of the time. During the day, they are in a dark room, with a special red or blue light source like those used in zoological gardens. The red or blue light source is different from regular light; it does not disrupt the hamster's sleep and reproductive patterns but it provides enough light to let you observe them while they are active in the dark.

In reality, reverse-light cycle conditions are very difficult to maintain except under laboratory conditions. If your hamsters are exposed to light, even for a brief moment, they revert to their nocturnal lifestyle. In order to maintain strict lighting conditions, you need to have special facilities and equipment. For the Chinese hamster, light cycle control and low noise levels are crucial environmental requirements for successful breeding programs. This is one of the reasons Chinese hamsters are difficult to raise in captivity.

Temperature and Humidity

Dwarf hamsters are quite comfortable at room temperature (69°F to 72°F [21°C to 22.2°C]). In fact, room temperature is close to the temperatures measured inside dwarf hamster burrows in the wild.

Hamsters should be protected from drafts, extreme fluctuations in temperature, and excessive dryness. Humidity should be no less than 40 percent in order to avoid dry skin problems and health problems. For baby hamsters, humidity should be at least 50 to 55 percent in order to prevent dehydration. Exchange of fresh air is also important. Hamsters need well-ventilated, but not drafty, enclosures. They should not be placed near heaters or fans, or in areas of direct sunlight. This is especially critical for animals housed in glass aquaria, because exposure to direct sunlight can raise temperatures beyond the comfort and safety zone (greenhouse effect). When temperatures reach the low 90s°F (approximately 33°C), dwarf hamsters quickly succumb to heatstroke and die.

Clean water bottles and provide fresh water daily. Check sipper tubes daily to make sure they are not plugged and are working correctly.

A running wheel with a solid floor is a necessity to allow dwarf hamsters plenty of exercise.

Houses and hide-aways are necessities to provide your pets with privacy and subdued lighting for their light-sensitive eyes. Wooden houses are perfect. They should be clean and made from non-treated, non-poisonous wood because your hamster will chew on them. They should be 3 to 4 inches wide × 6 inches long × 4 inches high (7.5 to 10 cm × 15 cm × 10 cm), to accommodate more than one dwarf hamster.

A dust bath should be provided in a shallow dish or bowl. You can use chinchilla dust, available from pet stores. Do not use other types of sand as they are too coarse and can damage hamster coats. Note: Not all hamsters will use a dust bath.

Most dwarf hamsters choose a specific corner of the cage to use for their toilet area. Once your pet has chosen a corner, keep that corner of the cage clear for that use only and do not put food or toys near the toilet corner.

Exercise

Hamsters need exercise. They work out in a variety of ways: sitting, standing, running, jumping, climbing, digging, and grooming.

If your hamster were out in the wild, it would cover a lot of ground, gather a lot of food, and dig a lot of tunnels during its waking hours. Since your hamster lives in a cage, it is up to you to be its recreational coordinator. This can be a fun job!

The types of activities you can provide your pet are limited only by your imagination.

Running Wheel

A running wheel is an excellent toy and provides lots of exercise. The running wheel should have a solid floor. Wire-floored running wheels are dangerous because hamsters can trap and injure their legs in the rungs. The wires can also hurt the hamsters' tiny, delicate feet. If your hamster seems to be obsessed with the running wheel and spends all its time in it, remove the wheel for a while. Offer your hamster other interesting toys to keep it busy, such as ladders, ramps, tube tunnels, and chew toys.

Hamster Balls and Hamster Cars

Hamster balls are clear plastic balls available from pet stores. They come apart so that a hamster can be placed enclosed inside the ball and run around inside of it. Most hamsters dislike these balls and similar toys, such as little hamster cars. Hamsters become frightened or panic when they are imprisoned inside of them. Although they have holes in them, there is not enough ventilation inside. It is easy for hamsters to panic and overheat inside of these devices. What may seem like an entertaining toy is actually cruel and inhumane treatment for some pets. Do *not* put your dwarf hamster in a hamster ball or toy car!

Tunnels and Tubes

Hamsters naturally enjoy tube and tunnel toys. For your pet's safety, be sure the diameter is wide enough to allow enough space to enter and play inside comfortably (at least 2 inches [2.5 cm] diameter). You don't have to spend a fortune on expensive, colorful tube systems from the pet store. You can make simple tube and tunnel toys from safe and inexpensive PVC available from your local hardware store. Keep the length short

so that there is adequate ventilation within the tubes and so they are easy to clean.

Dust Baths and Grooming

Some hamsters, especially Desert hamsters, enjoy cleaning the oil from their fur by rolling in dust baths. This simple pleasure is easy to provide for your pet (see HOW-TO: Cage Features, page 56).

Fortunately, hamsters are very good at grooming and keeping themselves clean. In fact, grooming is an important dwarf hamster ritual that takes place several times a day, usually immediately upon awakening. The animal often starts by raising one or both of its front legs over its head and pushing its fur forward with its front feet. It looks a bit like someone trying to pull a shirt off over his or her head. The hamster washes its face and fastidiously cleans its sides, hind legs, and feet. Grooming can take a long time and the hamster usually performs its grooming task in the same order every time it grooms. *One of the first signs of a problem or illness is that the hamster stops grooming.* You will notice that your hamsters spend a great deal of time grooming the fur around their scent glands. To us, hamsters are virtually odorless, but to hamsters, scent glands and odors play an important role in behavior, territoriality, and communication during breeding cycles. Not only do you not have to groom your hamster, but your hamster would object violently to your efforts! So there is no need to purchase any combs, brushes, or shampoos for these tiny creatures; in fact, a bath could cause

If your hamster escapes, look for it in every possible hiding place, including your shoes.

Dwarf hamster accessories: hideaways, exercise wheel, travel carrying case, and litter box.

a hamster to become chilled and sick. Shampoo products could also make your hamster ill. *Never use any shampoos or products containing pesticides to kill parasites on the skin.* These products are manufactured with larger animals, such as dogs or cats, in mind. The dose of active chemicals in these products could kill your hamster. Even shampoos that do not contain pesticides can be harmful to your pet. Besides, shampoos and perfumed grooming products will interfere with the hamster's natural scent gland odors and body oils.

If you think your hamster has a skin condition that needs attention, or that it may have parasites in its fur, contact your veterinarian. It is important to know exactly what the problem is. Your veterinarian can tell you if the problem is contagious to you, your hamsters, or your other pets. If treatment is required, your veterinarian will know which product to use and how much is safe to use on such a small animal. This is very important, since hamsters are very sensitive to many medications.

Toys for Dwarf Hamsters

Because hamsters are very active, curious animals, toys are a worthwhile investment in your pet's overall enrichment and well-being. They stimulate your pet to explore and play. Toys such as running wheels, wire ladders, ramps, tunnels and tubes provide entertainment for both you and your pet. Hamsters love to chew. Because their front teeth grow continually and must be worn down, they should be provided with safe rodent chew toys. It is safest to purchase rodent chew sticks from a pet store. If you give your hamster wooden chew sticks, be sure that these materials do not have sharp points or edges that can injure the sensitive cheek pouches. Remember that whatever toys you select, your pet will chew on

them, so be sure they are made of nontoxic materials, are not chemically treated, and are not constructed from toxic plants.

Household Hazards

One of the most delightful features about dwarf hamsters—their diminutive size—also creates some of the biggest problems for their safety. They are able to fit through spaces one would never think possible. If they can squeeze their head through any crack, the rest of the body follows easily. For this reason, it is not safe to house them in cages with bars, unless the bars are very close together. It is also impossible to keep a hamster in a wood or cardboard container because it will chew its way out. Even holding a busy hamster can be a challenge, as it can squeeze between fingers or jump and bounce out of your palms, and once your hamster is loose, it faces countless life-threatening situations in your home.

Capturing a runaway hamster can be extremely difficult to accomplish and takes some time. If your hamster escapes, you need to know what potential household hazards it may encounter so you can correct the situation in advance.

Sticky Traps and Snap Traps

Go through your house and look at it from your hamster's point of view. Look for any cracks, spaces, or holes that your hamster can crawl into, as well as anything it can fall into where it can be trapped. If you have any sticky or snap traps set in your house or garage, pick them up immediately—they are as deadly for your pet as they are for wild rodents.

Household Chemicals

Hamsters like to crawl into cabinets where there are often household products such as cleaning agents, insect sprays, paints, fertilizers, pesticide baits, and other poisonous chemicals.

Linoleum floors and some types of decking contain arsenic. All of these substances are extremely dangerous and potentially deadly for your pet if it comes in contact with them. Some types of paints can be toxic to your pet if it chews on wooden baseboards or walls, and wood splinters or sharp foreign objects can injure the soft lining of your hamster's cheek pouches. Because hamsters are so tiny it takes only a small amount of poison to kill them.

Electrical Shock

Unplug and remove any electrical cords that may be within reach of your escaped hamster. Electrocution from gnawing on an electrical cord is a danger that could cost your pet its life and possibly cause an electrical fire.

Appliances

Before you do the laundry, check your clothing, especially the pockets. A laundry basket makes a warm hiding place for a snoozing hamster. More than one of these little animals have been found, too late, inside the washer or dryer.

Toxic Plants

While your little escapee is on the loose, it may get hungry and sample some greenery in your home or garden. Unfortunately, most ornamental plants are poisonous, so be sure to remove any plants, fertilizers, and pesticides that could make your pet sick.

Common poisonous plants include:
- Aconite
- African violet
- Amaryllis
- American holly
- American nightshade
- Angel's trumpet
- Azalea
- Bird of paradise
- Birdseye primrose
- Blue cardinal flower (lobelia)
- Buttercup (ranunculus)
- Chrysanthemum
- Crocus
- Daffodil
- Daily
- Dieffenbachia
- Ficus
- Foxglove (digitalis)
- Hydrangea
- Iris
- Lily (several species of lily)
- Lupine
- Mistletoe
- Monkshood
- Oleander
- Onion
- Philodendron
- Poinsettia
- Rhododendron
- Tulip
- Wolfsbane
- Yew

Pets

If you have other pets in the house, remember that they pose a serious threat to your hamster. A gentle dog or curious cat quickly regains its instincts to hunt or kill small prey, especially when stimulated by the sight of a small animal trying to flee. A fatal accident can take place in a split second. There will also be less chance of your hamster coming out of its hiding place if it senses there are other animals in the area, so, until your hamster is recovered, put your other pets in a secure place where

Always keep your dwarf hamster safe and protected from other animals.

they cannot hurt your hamster when it does finally come out of hiding.

If there are small children in your home, ask their assistance in finding the hamster. Children are very eager to be helpful and are remarkably skilled at finding the smallest things—but remind the child not to touch the animal when it is found. A startled hamster can inflict a serious bite wound. Also, a small child may inadvertently frighten your pet away, or step on it, before you arrive and capture it.

Outside Doors

Make sure all doors to the outside or garage are closed. If your hamster escapes outside it will be virtually impossible to find it and it will certainly not survive the dangers of automobiles, neighborhood animals, wild animals, birds of prey, or exposure.

Crushing Injuries

If, despite your efforts to keep your pet in its cage, it escapes, the first thing everyone in the house must do is be careful where they step; your hamster can dart out from under an object and be underfoot before you know it. Hamsters also like to hide in dark places, so inspect your closets and the insides of your shoes. Check your furniture before you sit down on it. Hamsters love to tunnel through cushions and fabrics and may even be found inside a couch, chair, or pillow.

Capturing Your Hamster

Be prepared to capture your hamster when you do find it by having a can or a small box available to quickly place over it. If this technique seems too cumbersome for you, try using a thick cloth, such as a hand towel, to throw over your pet like a net. Once the cloth is over the hamster, you must act quickly to roll the hamster up in the towel or cover it with a box or can.

You can also purchase a small humane trap at the local pet shop or feed store. If you cannot purchase a trap, you may be able to rent or borrow one from the local animal shelter. Bait the trap with your hamster's favorite treat and place it in an easily accessible, quiet area, with subdued lighting.

If all else fails, you can make a safe and inexpensive homemade trap:

✔ Simply place a treat in a large coffee can or a small bucket, or deep plastic box.

✔ Tilt a small ramp made of wood, cardboard, screen, mesh, or plastic against the container and bait the ramp with treats so the hamster will continue to climb the ramp as it follows the path of treats.

✔ Tilt the ramp in such a way that when your hamster climbs to the top of the ramp, it will also be at the top of the container. Following its sense of smell, your pet might slide in after the bait but will not be able to climb up the smooth sides of the container.

If you are using a trap, you are most likely to catch your hamster during the evening when it is active. It will probably be hidden and sleeping during the day.

Whatever kind of traps you use, be sure to check them several times a day. By the time you catch your hamster, it may be very hungry and thirsty and may need immediate care.

You can make a humane trap to catch your escaped hamster, using a bucket, a ramp, and a treat.

HOW-TO: CAGE FEATURES

Recommended Cage Features

Select a cage large enough to accommodate all your hamsters plus their houses, toys, dishes, bottle, and running wheel. Cages should be nonporous, easy to clean, chew-proof, and escape-proof. Plexiglas, stainless steel, or durable plastic work well. If you buy a stainless steel wire cage, be sure that the bars are horizontal, rather than vertical, to reduce chances of injury. Bars should be close enough (1/3 inch [7 mm]) to prevent escape. Wooden caging is not recommended because it is difficult to clean and hamsters can chew their way out of them. Wire cage floors are not recommended because they are hard on delicate dwarf hamster feet and can injure them. A standard 10-gallon (38-L) glass aquarium, with an escape-proof screen or wire-mesh lid, makes an excellent cage. The glass walls provide protection from drafts and give a clear view of your hamsters.

Hamsters can do well in plastic shoebox-shaped cages if they are not too small. These cages have snap-on stainless steel tops with space for water bottles and food. Be sure that the sipper tube of the water bottle is long enough for your hamsters to reach, especially the babies. You may have to purchase an extra-long sipper tube.

If you purchase a cage with a wire bottom, make sure the wire sits directly on the floor pan and cover it with bedding material.

Wire-bottom cages are messy because hamsters push the shavings about and they can scatter outside of the cage. If you must use a wire-bottom cage, make sure the bottom is well covered in bedding and place the cage inside a floor pan 3 to 4 inches (8 to 10 cm) deep to prevent messes.

No matter what type of cage you select, it should allow adequate ventilation and be large enough to prevent overcrowding. The cage should be no smaller than 20 inches long × 12 inches wide × 16 inches high (50 cm × 30 cm × 40 cm), preferably much larger for a small group of dwarf hamsters. Ideally, the height of the aquarium should be 32 inches (80 cm), because dwarf hamsters are nimble climbers and jumpers and great escape artists. Make sure the lid fastens securely. The cage should always be large enough so that you can use both hands to gently scoop up your hamsters.

Bedding Material

Wood shavings make good bedding material. Aspen or alder shavings are recommended. Avoid cedar shavings, as they contain oils that can cause health problems such as allergies, itchy skin, scratching, and even liver problems. Pine shavings also contain oils that can make hamsters sick, although some manufacturers claim their pine shavings are processed to be safe for small pets, so check packaging information carefully. Wood chips should be avoided, as they have sharp particles that can injure a dwarf hamster's delicate eyes. Dwarf hamster bedding should be as dust-free as possible, so it does not irritate the animals' delicate nasal passages and lungs and cause wheezing, sneezing, and other respiratory problems. For this reason, sawdust (and compressed pellets that break down into sawdust when damp) is *not* recommended for use as hamster bedding material.

Only wood shavings that are packaged and indicated for use as bedding material for caged pets should be used in your hamster's cage. Shavings sold for horse stalls or stored in open outdoor bins may be contaminated with urine and disease-causing organisms from wild rodents. Shavings absorb urine and odors and should be changed at least once a week. If several animals are housed together, replace bedding twice a week or more often as necessary.

Nesting Material

Hamsters love to build nests. Female hamsters that build the most elaborate nests are often the most successful in raising their young. The presence of sufficient nesting material in the cage also appears to prevent the mother from cannibalizing her pups.

If your hamster has pups, do not change or remove the nesting material. You can provide fresh material for her to arrange as she pleases, but disturbing the nest will upset her. Leave all nesting material alone.

There are several kinds of nesting material available. Shredded paper is one of the best, most popular, and least expensive. Use only shredded paper available commercially for hamster cages. Do not use shredded paper from an office and do not use shredded newspaper, as these may contain toxic inks. Colored commercial paper bedding makes the cage bright and interesting, but white bedding material enables you to detect abnormally colored urine or the presence of blood, in case of injury. Colored paper may stain your hamster's coat when the bedding gets wet.

Nesting material should be clean and safe for your pet. Fluffy nesting material from synthetic fabrics or cotton wool is not safe because hamsters can become caught or tangled in it, or choke on the material. It is difficult to remove from their cheek pouches. Fluffy nesting material can cause intestinal obstruction and death because it cannot be digested. Hay can be used for nesting material, but it should be fresh, purchased commercially, packaged for use in pet cages, and not contain dust or mold.

A dust bath in the home is a special treat.

Make sure the sipper tube is low enough for the babies to reach, but not so low it touches the bedding material.

FEEDING YOUR DWARF HAMSTER

Dwarf hamsters are not fussy eaters. They enjoy a wide variety of plants, seeds, grains, fruits, and vegetables. It is easy and fun to give your tiny friend a well-balanced diet!

In the wild, the dwarf hamster's diet consists of whatever seasonal seeds, grasses, leaves, and insects it can find and hoard. In captivity, dwarf hamsters should be fed a fresh, clean, nutritious, and tasty diet.

Feeding Habits

Dwarf hamsters are hoarding animals by nature. They enjoy removing food from one location to another, filling their cheek pouches to maximum capacity, and depositing the contents in a corner of the cage floor. These interesting habits cannot be changed or stopped. Dwarf hamsters are very tidy and usually soil only one corner of their cage. They are careful to place their food in piles or corners away from the corner they have used for urination and defecation. You can help prevent unsanitary food conditions by changing the cage and bedding regularly.

Because of your pet's forage and storage behavior, feed bowls and feeders are not necessary. Dwarf hamsters have difficulty using feeders and all will relocate their food to a corner on the cage floor. If you decide to use feeders or bowls, they should be made of nontoxic, nonchewable material, such as ceramic or stainless steel and cleaned daily.

What to Feed

Dwarf hamsters thrive on the large selection of pelleted hamster diets commercially available from pet stores. A complete pelleted diet with more than 14 percent protein content provides adequate nutrition for dwarf hamsters. Many hamster diets contain 22 percent protein to support all aspects of growth, reproduction, gestation, lactation, and maintenance. From information obtained from laboratory rodents, it is probable a diet consisting of 18 to 19 percent protein more closely approximates the hamster's daily requirement.

Commercial Hamster Food

Balanced nutrition plays an important role in your pet's overall health, life span, and reproduction. The majority of the diet should consist of high-quality commercial hamster food. Be

sure to check the milling or manufacture date of the food, which should be located on the side or back of the box. If hamster food sits too long on a shelf, many of the vitamins and nutrients lose their potency. Be sure the food you provide is fresh and check daily to be certain the food is free of mold or vermin. Store the food in airtight, closed containers in a cool, dry place.

Do not feed your hamster diets manufactured for other species. For example, do not feed your hamster rat, mouse, chinchilla, ferret, rabbit, cat, or dog food. The food ingredients, including vitamin and mineral supplementations, are formulated to meet the special needs of the species for which they are manufactured. Dog and cat foods contain artificial colors, flavor additives, and preservatives, and are high in fat and salt content. Corn is often a key ingredient in dog and cat foods, so they are high in carbohydrates. They can lead to obesity, diabetes, nutritional imbalance, and gastric upset in dwarf hamsters. Dog and cat

foods are designed for carnivores, not for herbivore/insectivore rodents. *Feed your dwarf hamster commercial food developed for hamsters only!*

Birdseed and Insects

In the wild, dwarf hamsters eat a variety of seeds and insects. Your pet will enjoy a small treat of birdseed or insects once in a while. It is safest to feed your hamster only insects purchased from a pet store, such as small crickets and mealworms. Be sure to buy small mealworms. They come in a plastic container and will stay alive for several days.

Fruits and Vegetables

Years ago it was observed that female hamsters in breeding colonies raised larger litters when they were given a raw vegetable supplement. This was determined to be due to the moisture the vegetables provided the young hamsters that were not yet able to reach the sipper tubes of their water bottles. By lowering the sipper tubes to ½ inch to ¾ inch (13 to 19 mm) above the cage bedding, where the baby hamsters could reach them, an increase in pup survival was achieved. You can also provide the pups with moisture by giving them a very small piece of fresh apple.

Your pet will enjoy a small amount of fresh fruit or raw vegetables (hamsters love carrots!) as a special treat once in a while, but be sure not to overdo it. Dwarf hamsters should be given fruits and vegetables in small quantities for several reasons:

✔ Dwarf hamsters prefer to eat fruits and vegetables and will ignore their nutritionally balanced commercial diet.

✔ Too many fruits and vegetables can cause intestinal upset and diarrhea.

✔ Excess nuts, especially peanuts, are high in fat content and can lead to obesity.

✔ Excess fruits and sugars cause dental caries, obesity, and diabetes in hamsters.

✔ Some fruits and vegetables may cause symptoms suggestive of food allergies. For example, corn causes itchy, dry skin in some animals.

If you wish to give your pet a special treat, do it infrequently and in small quantities. Remember to remove any uneaten fruits and vegetables from the cage before they spoil. A combination of fresh hamster food pellets, with an occasional special treat of insects, raw vegetables, or fruits, make mealtime interesting and nutritious.

How Much and How Often

Dwarf hamsters are very small, but they are also eager eaters. What your pet does not eat immediately, it will store away to eat at a later time. It is difficult to know exactly how much your hamster has eaten in a day because some of the food may be hidden in piles or in the bedding. On average your hamster will eat ¼ ounce (5 to 7 g) of food daily. That is not very much, but then, your pet is not very large. If you overfeed your hamster, you will notice its storage piles becoming higher and higher. Remove old food so that it does not become contaminated or spoiled.

If your dwarf hamster does not have much food stashed away and it appears thin, inactive, or in poor health, then feed it more food. Keep in mind that dwarf hamsters that are very active, pregnant, lactating, ill, or housed in cool environments, need more food than hamsters that are not subjected to these stresses.

Dwarf hamsters are most active in the evening and early morning, so if you wish to keep in step with your pet's natural schedule, feed it in the evening.

Vitamins and Minerals

If your pet is receiving a quality commercial hamster diet, it is usually unnecessary to supplement the diet with vitamins, minerals, and salt blocks. Indiscriminate supplementation can be harmful.

Potentially Harmful Foods

Foods that are sharp, dry, stiff, or sticky (such as candy or dried fruits) can lodge in the cheek pouches or injure the delicate tissue of the mouth. Avoid these foods.

Do not feed your pet cooked or processed foods, chocolate (which contains theobromine, a product similar to caffeine), or other candies, or "junk food."

Do not give your pet foods high in sugar content. These foods cause dental caries (cavities, decay), obesity, diabetes, and other health problems in dwarf hamsters.

Grapes and raisins are high in sugar content and have been documented to cause kidney failure and death in some animal species. To be safe, do not feed your hamsters grapes and raisins.

Do not feed your hamster the green parts or sprouts ("eyes") of a potato. These contain a poison called *solanine* that can kill your pet.

If you are not sure about the safety or nutritional benefit of any food type, simply play it safe—do not feed it to your pet.

Nutritional Disorders

Rodent nutritional requirements have been studied extensively and are available from publications of the National Academy of Sciences and various feed companies. If dwarf hamsters are not fed a balanced diet, they may suffer from a wide range of medical problems.

A common nutritional problem observed in hamsters is vitamin E deficiency. Signs include weak muscles in young and adult hamsters. Vitamin E deficiency also causes diminished reproduction and a central nervous system disorder called Spontaneous Hemorrhagic Necrosis (SHN), which affects unborn (fetal) and newborn hamsters. The problem is caused by feeding the mother hamster a diet deficient in vitamin E during her pregnancy. Most commercial diets are supplemented with vitamin E.

Vitamin D, together with the photoperiod, plays an important role in dwarf hamster reproduction (in particular, the Siberian hamster, *Phodopus sungorus*) by influencing hormone levels and testicular growth. Vitamin D also affects the hamster's metabolism and immune system.

Ensuring that the commercial hamster diet you purchase is fresh and has not exceeded its shelf life will eliminate the risk of feeding your hamster a product that has lost its nutritional value.

Water

Depending on location, the contents of city water or well water vary and could contain additives such as chlorine and chloramine, high levels of undesirable elements, such as arsenic, or low levels of bacteria. Recent research has shown that fluoride can help prevent dental caries in dwarf hamsters, but this is in laboratory studies only. The amount of fluoride in city water that comes out of your faucet might not be a safe level for your hamster. The best water you can provide your pet is the same

drinking water you buy for yourself. Do not give your pet distilled, demineralized, deionized, or carbonated water. Animals require natural minerals found in spring water. Commercial bottled drinking water is an inexpensive and safe way to keep your pet healthy.

Be aware of the following:

✔ Dwarf hamsters should have access to pure, clean drinking water at all times. Water is especially important because much of the hamster's diet is dry (pellets, seeds), increasing the animal's need for water.

✔ The water bottle should be cleaned, rinsed well, and refilled daily. Pay particular attention to cleaning the sipper tube, which can become clogged with small particles and harbor bacteria.

✔ A small hamster can drink up to one sixth of an ounce (5 ml, or one teaspoon) of water daily. Water intake depends on activity level, health condition, age, and reproductive activity. If your hamster is pregnant or nursing babies, she may drink more than twice the amount of water she usually does. Ambient temperature and humid-

ity also affect water consumption. Animals housed in a warm, dry room will drink more than those in cooler, more humid environments.

✔ Always provide more water than your hamster normally drinks.

✔ Check the sipper tube to be certain it is functioning properly.

✔ If you have baby hamsters ten days of age or older, they must have access to drinking water. Lower their water bottle so that the sipper tube is ½ inch to ¾ inch (13 to 19 mm) above the cage bedding, within their reach. Check frequently to see that the sipper tube has not come in contact with the cage bedding. If this happens, the sipper tube can either become plugged or the water may completely wick out into the bedding material.

✔ As a precaution against dehydration, provide moisture for your pups in case there is a water bottle accident during your absence. Leave a small amount of fresh, raw, moist vegetable (carrot, lettuce). Remember to check all hiding places and discard old food so it does not rot.

HEALTH

Hamsters are hardy, resilient little creatures, but they must have very good care to remain healthy into their old age. Check your hamster every day. If your pet is sick, it needs immediate help to ensure its survival.

Keeping Hamsters Healthy

The most important health care you can provide your hamster is preventive health care—preventing problems is much easier than treating problems.

Sometimes even the best-cared-for animals become ill. Successful recovery depends upon the illness and how early it was detected and treated. To recognize a sick hamster, you must first know how a healthy hamster looks and acts. If your pet is acting sluggish, has a poor coat, hunched-up posture, or is not eating, then there is most certainly a problem. The sooner you begin treatment, the better your pet's chances of recovery.

If Your Hamster Is Sick

1. The first thing you should do the moment you notice your pet is ill is separate it from any other pets you have so that, if the problem is contagious, you have reduced the chances of spreading disease to your other animals.

2. Isolate your sick hamster to give it a chance to begin its recuperation in peace and quiet without the stress and competition of other hamsters.

3. Place your hamster in a comfortable, dark, quiet place.

4. Continue to keep a close watch on your other hamsters and separate any others that may also become ill.

5. Wash thoroughly all housing, toys, dishes, and bottles that were in contact with your sick pet. Discard old food and used bedding and nesting material.

6. Wash your hands thoroughly after handling any sick animal and before handling other pets or food. This will help prevent the possible spread of contagious disease.

7. Contact your veterinarian for advice. An examination is important to diagnose the problem. It is the only way to know exactly what the problem is and whether it is contagious to you or your other pets. A prescription medication may be indicated to ensure your pet's survival. Hamsters are sensitive to some medications, so your veterinarian's expertise is necessary. Because handling and transportation can be too stressful for your sick pet, your veterinarian may make a house call, but if you must transport your hamster, it is less stressful if the hamster can travel in a small cage. Cover the cage with a cloth to reduce sounds and light that can startle your pet.

A sick hamster is lethargic and depressed. Its condition can quickly deteriorate without proper treatment.

Helping Your Veterinarian Help You

Make a list of all the questions you want to ask your veterinarian. Your veterinarian will also ask you some questions to help make a diagnosis and determine an appropriate treatment. Don't worry if you don't have all the answers—every piece of information will be helpful for your pet.

Before your appointment, make a list of the answers to the following questions:

1. How old is your hamster?

2. How long have you owned your pet?

3. What species is your hamster?

4. When did you first notice the problem?

5. Does your pet appear to be in any discomfort or pain?

6. What, if anything, have you given or done to treat the problem?

7. When did your hamster last eat or drink?

8. Has there been a change in your pet's diet or living environment?

9. When did your hamster last have a bowel movement? Was it normal, constipated, or diarrhea?

10. Are there any other animals at home? If so, what kind and how many?

11. How many animals are housed in the same cage with your sick hamster?

12. If you have any other pets, did you purchase any of them recently?

13. Do any of your other pets have any problems that seem similar or related?

14. What do you feed your hamster (including special treats)?

15. How is your hamster housed?

16. What is the cage-cleaning schedule?

17. Has your pet been exposed to any sick animals or chemicals?

18. Where did you obtain your pet?

Ways to Tell If Your Hamster Is Healthy

	Healthy Hamster	Sick Hamster
Appearance	Bright, clear eyes	Dull expression; eyes partially closed
	Well-groomed, shiny coat	Untidy, dull, ruffled coat; soiling around anus/genitals
	Stocky; compact	Thin; losing weight
Behavior	Curious and alert	Lethargic; depressed
	Active and lively	Slow; unwilling to move
	Forages and plays	Does not explore or play
	Good appetite	Will not eat or drink
	Standing, running, sitting	Hunched-up position

19. If your hamster is a female, is she pregnant or when did she last produce a litter?

20. Add any other findings or relevant information.

Health Problems

Hamsters can contract a variety of bacterial, viral, and fungal infections. They may be troubled by external (skin, hair, ears) and internal (intestinal) parasites. They may also suffer from noncontagious medical conditions, such as cancer, diabetes, and genetic disorders.

People and animals can share or spread the same germs. If your hamster becomes ill, your veterinarian can answer questions you may have about the contagion of different diseases or parasites.

Zoonoses

Zoonoses are diseases that can be transmitted between humans and animals. Lymphocytic choriomeningitis virus (LCMV) is spread by some rodents, such as wild mice, to humans. LCMV can also be transmitted from mice to other rodents, and possibly to dwarf hamsters. LCMV usually does not cause illness except in people with weak immune systems, or in pregnant women (the virus can seriously harm the developing fetus). Although other hamster species have been reported to carry LCMV, the American Medical Association states that at this time there is insufficient information to know the potential for LCMV infection in dwarf hamsters.

Bite Wounds

Bite wounds are one of the most common types of injuries that occur in hamsters. The incidence of bite wounds can be reduced by housing animals separately and by not overcrowding them. Bite wounds can become infected and form abscesses.

To check your hamster for bite wounds, push the fur back with your fingers and look for any

To prevent escape and injury, always keep the lid securely fastened on your pet's cage.

lumps, bumps, puncture holes, swelling, redness, tenderness, or pus. If a bite wound is deep, it can cause muscle and nerve damage.

Treatment: Clean the wound with a mild antiseptic solution or hydrogen peroxide. Keep the wound clean and allow it to drain until it has closed and healed. Use paper bedding material and avoid shavings until healed.

Cheek Pouch Injury

Cheek pouches can be injured by sharp objects or impacted with some kinds of fluffy bedding material or foreign objects. If your hamster is unable to empty its cheek pouches, they could be swollen, inflamed, impacted, infected, or obstructed with foreign objects. Contact your veterinarian immediately.

Dehydration

Dehydration occurs when an animal loses too much water from the body. There are many causes of dehydration, including not drinking enough water, illness, diarrhea, and exposure to a hot environment.

Treatment: The treatment for dehydration is rehydration, which is replenishing the body with water. When an animal becomes dehydrated, it also loses minerals from its body. A balanced electrolyte solution is a mixture of water and necessary minerals in the proper dilution for rehydration. Electrolyte solutions are available from your veterinarian. In an emergency, you can also find electrolyte solutions formulated for human babies, available at pharmacies and supermarkets. Keep a bottle on hand in case of emergency.

Note: Do not give your pet homemade salt or sugar mixtures without consulting your veterinarian. In the wrong proportions, these will do more harm than good by further dehydrating your pet.

Dental Problems

The outer surface of the incisors is harder than the inside material, so as your hamster chews, its teeth are constantly chiseled and sharpened. There are no nerves in the incisors, except at the base of the tooth where growth takes place.

Check your hamster's mouth regularly for dental problems. Grasp your hamster firmly by the nape of the neck, pulling the loose cheek pouch skin back from around its mouth to reveal the front incisors.

Most dental problems can be avoided by providing safe chew toys, a balanced diet sufficient in calcium content, and by removing animals with dental problems from the breeding program.

Malocclusion: When the incisors do not grow or align as they should, the teeth wear unevenly. This is called *malocclusion*, and is usually an inherited problem. One or more of the misdirected incisors may grow into the roof of the mouth or into the delicate lining of the cheek pouches. This painful condition eventually makes it difficult or impossible for the hamster to eat. Signs of malocclusion include protruding teeth, lack of appetite, weight loss, and swollen, painful mouth and cheek pouches.

Treatment: The offending tooth may be trimmed back to the correct length. Because your hamster is so tiny, it is easy to break its jaw or cut its tongue, lips, or cheeks if great care is not taken during the procedure. This is a job for your veterinarian. No anesthetic is required because there is no sensation in the distal end of the tooth. The tooth will grow back and will need to be trimmed regularly. Hamsters that have dental malocclusion should not be used for breeding.

Broken teeth: Sometimes an incisor may break. It will grow back, but during that time the tooth opposite the missing or broken tooth may become overgrown because it has nothing to grind against. You may need to trim the opposite tooth until the broken tooth grows back.

Tooth and gum infection: Once in a while, a tooth may become infected or require removal. Your hamster may have a swollen mouth and refuse to eat. Dental extraction is a job for your veterinarian!

Ear Problems

It is not always easy to tell if your hamster is having problems with its ears, since it is diffi-cult to see inside the ear canal. Ear problems may be caused by parasites, infection, or injury. Signs of ear problems include scratching at the ears, head shaking, tilting the head to one side, and loss of balance.

Treatment: Place a drop of mineral oil on a cotton-tipped swab and gently wipe away any dirt or debris from your hamster's ears. This may also give your pet some relief from itching. Contact your veterinarian.

Eye Problems

Eye problems may develop from injury, infection, or irritating substances. Check your pet daily to be sure its eyes are clear and bright. If your hamster's eyes are dull, have a discharge, or are closed, place your hamster in a dark room and contact your veterinarian. Many eye problems are painful or sensitive to light. Your veterinarian can provide an appropriate, gentle eyewash and eye ointment or drops if necessary.

Many eye problems look similar; for example, ulcers of the cornea and cataracts both give the eyes a cloudy appearance. Some eye problems cannot be treated or may be signs of additional health problems; for example, cataracts are frequently seen in diabetic animals. Anophthalmia,

Hamsters are very clean and groom themselves several times a day.

or the absence of eyes, is often an inherited condition.

Treatment: Many eye conditions are very painful, and most require veterinary expertise, so contact your veterinarian immediately. Light may hurt your hamster's eyes, so place it in a dark room until your veterinary appointment. Unfortunately, there is no treatment or cure for anophthalmia.

Gastrointestinal Problems

Stomach and intestinal problems can be caused by bacterial or viral infections, parasites, inadequate nutrition, sudden change of diet, stress, or poor housing conditions. These problems are often painful conditions and can cause constipation or diarrhea.

Constipation: Constipation is difficulty passing dry, hard feces. Causes of constipation include dehydration, insufficient water intake, dry or hot environment, an exclusively dry diet, obstruction of the intestinal tract, and parasitism.

Treatment: Be sure your hamster can reach the water bottle and that the sipper tube is functioning properly. Remove all dry food and give your hamster moist food, such as apple or lettuce, and contact your veterinarian right away.

Diarrhea: Diarrhea is a very serious condition in hamsters. Among its many causes are disease, stress, change in diet, or an excess of fruits and vegetables in the diet. Diarrhea causes rapid dehydration and death if not treated quickly. The feces are soft, mucous, or liquid and may have a foul odor. "Wet tail" is a general term used to describe diarrhea in the hamster, because hamsters with diarrhea are often wet and soiled around the anus and tail.

Treatment: If your hamster has diarrhea, it may need medicine to recover. Stop feeding any fruits or vegetables and ask your veterinarian for a balanced electrolyte solution for rehydration. Isolate hamsters with diarrhea from other hamsters, as diarrhea may be caused by contagious bacteria or viruses.

Heatstroke

Hamsters do not tolerate heat well and can become overheated in a very short time. Be sure that your hamster's cage is not in direct sunlight and is not close to any fireplaces or heaters. If you must transport you pet, never leave it in the car. On a warm day, a car can heat up to 120°F (48.9°C) in a few minutes, even with the windows partially open. Adequate ventilation is also important to prevent your pet from becoming too hot.

If your hamster is exposed to high temperatures, it will try to cool off by lying spread out flat on its belly. It will quickly become weak, unresponsive, and eventually comatose. Without immediate emergency treatment, it will die. You will have to quickly and safely lower your hamster's temperature. Then you will have to rehydrate your pet.

Treatment: To cool down your hamster, hold it in your hand in a sink of cool (not cold) water. Be sure to keep its head above water so it can safely breathe. Once your hamster has regained consciousness, dry it gently and place it in a dry, dark, comfortable cage to rest. Next,

rehydrate your hamster with a balanced electrolyte solution, using a plastic eyedropper to deliver the solution. Make sure your hamster is fully conscious and able to swallow so that the solution does not go into its lungs.

Injury and Trauma

Little animals have a way of sometimes being in the wrong place at the wrong time. If your hamster is dropped, stepped on, sat upon, or injured in any way, try to determine how seriously it is hurt. Isolate it in a clean, comfortable cage. Do not handle your hamster more than necessary. Observe it closely to be sure it acts and moves about normally and continues to eat and drink. Contact your veterinarian for advice.

Nails: Busy hamsters usually keep their nails worn down. If a nail is too long, or overgrown, it can snag on something, tear, and bleed. Unless the nail bed has been damaged, the nail will grow back, but, in the meantime, the injury should be kept clean to prevent infection.

Treatment: Long nails can be trimmed using small nail clippers designed for human babies. The blood supply to the nail begins where the nail changes color from white to pink, near the base of the toenail. When you trim your pet's nails, just trim the very tips and do not trim the pink area.

Rectal prolapse: When the intestines become very inflamed, they may swell and protrude from the anus. The prolapsed rectum looks like a red tube sticking out of the body. This is a painful condition. If the swelling is not too great, the intestine can sometimes be gently pushed back into the body. Often, however, the intestine will prolapse again, shortly after it has been replaced. The problem can sometimes be

Fresh water is important. For keeping in easy reach, a longer sipper tube can be purchased.

corrected by surgery. Treatment for rectal prolapse in the hamster is usually not successful.

Respiratory Problems

If you hear your hamster wheezing or sneezing, take these symptoms seriously and contact your veterinarian immediately. Your pet may have developed an allergy, or fine, powdery bedding may be irritating its respiratory tract. In more serious cases, your hamster may have been exposed to dangerous germs, or to a damp, cold, drafty environment. Whatever the initial cause, your hamster could develop pneu-

monia. Signs of pneumonia include breathing difficulty, discharge from the eyes and nose, lack of appetite, inactivity, and weight loss. Hamsters seldom recover from pneumonia, even with proper medication.

Skin and Fur Problems

Signs of skin problems include: loss of fur, sores, dry, flaky, itchy skin, and moist, oozing, reddened skin. Skin problems may be caused by tiny skin parasites, allergies, hormonal imbalance, improper diet, disease, or fungal and bacterial infections. The exact cause of your pet's condition must be diagnosed by your veterinarian. Often, a specific prescription medication is required to treat the problem successfully.

Loss of fur does not always indicate a problem. Shedding is a normal event during warm weather. Mother hamsters shed fur around their teats when they are nursing their young. When cool weather returns, hamsters grow a new coat. Old hamsters have thin coats and less fur due to a drop in certain hormone levels as they age.

Scent Glands

The mid-ventral scent glands can become inflamed, infected, or scab. They should be gently cleaned with warm water and a mild antiseptic solution. Do not use cleaning solutions that contain alcohol—they sting!

Unavoidable Problems

Some medical conditions, such as problems with the heart, kidneys, liver, or other internal organs, may go unnoticed. Many problems associated with aging or genetics, such as diabetes or cancer, cannot be prevented. If your

pet has a medical problem you cannot treat or cure, you can still provide the best home care of all—good food and a safe, comfortable, loving home.

Normal Conditions Commonly Mistaken for Problems

Hamsters have some normal conditions that are often mistaken for problems. Don't let these little creatures fool you!

✔ Filled cheek pouches—sometimes mistaken for swelling or disease

✔ Scent glands—mistaken for a sore or injury on the belly or flank

✔ Large scrotum—mistaken for swelling or tumor

✔ Urine—normal hamster urine is yellow and thick, often mistaken for pus

✔ Vaginal discharge—normal discharge present the day after estrus is yellow and thick and often mistaken for pus

Sensitivity to Medications

Hamsters are very sensitive to some types of medicine. Many antibiotics can cause severe allergic reactions and sudden death. The list of antibiotics known to be toxic for hamsters is very long and includes penicillins, cephalosporins, dihydrostreptomycin, streptomycin, erythromycin, tetracycline, chlortetracycline, lincomycin, and vancomycin, to name only a few.

Never give your hamster any medicine intended for you, family members, or your other pets. Use only medicines prescribed for your hamster by your veterinarian and give no more than the recommended dose.

Dwarf Hamster Health Check Sheet

Health Problem	Symptoms	Causes
Bite wounds	Sores; redness; swelling; infection; pain or tenderness; draining pus	Fighting among incompatible animals; overcrowding; not enough hiding places in cage
Broken teeth	Tooth breaks and tooth opposite broken tooth grows too long, invades mouth tissue; inability to eat; pain	Trauma; old age; insufficient calcium in diet; chewing hard objects
Cheek pouch injury	Cheek pouches are swollen, impacted, or infected, and painful when touched; hamster is unable to empty cheek pouches	Access to sharp objects that can injure mouth, or fluffy bedding or pasty foods that can stick in cheek pouches; broken teeth
Constipation	Straining to pass hard, dry feces or inability to pass feces; depression, lethargy; hunched-up position; dry, ruffled fur	Insufficient water intake; dehydration; hot, dry environment; obstruction of intestinal tract; internal parasites; disease
Dehydration	Skin is stiff and lacks elasticity; skin pulled from the nape of the neck or back stands up stiffly or is slow to return to normal position; hamster sits in a hunched-up position; lethargic and weak	Bacterial or viral infections and diseases; stress; change in diet; too many fruits and vegetables in diet; heatstroke, diarrhea
Dental malocclusion	Protruding front teeth; lack of appetite; inability to eat; weight loss; swollen, painful mouth and cheek pouches; infection	Genetically inherited condition where teeth grow in wrong direction; may also be due to trauma or injury to mouth or teeth
Diarrhea	Soft, mucous, or liquid feces; bad odor; wetness around anus, tail, and belly	Disease; dehydration; stress; change in diet; too many fruits and vegetables
Ear problems	Scratching; head shaking; loss of balance; irritability upon handling	Parasites; infection; injury; disease

Do	Don't
Cleanse wounds with antiseptic, one part hydrogen peroxide diluted with three parts water; keep clean; allow to drain	Do not overcrowd or house animals that are not compatible with each other
Trim tooth opposite broken tooth until broken tooth has grown back to normal length and both teeth mesh properly	Do not allow the opposite tooth to grow into soft tissues of the mouth
Examine mouth for cause of problem; remove any foreign objects; trim overgrown teeth; consult veterinarian	Do not allow access to sharp objects, fluffy bedding, or pasty foods; do not allow poorly aligned teeth to grow too long
Determine possible cause; increase fluid intake; observe for possible bowel obstruction; check for parasites	Do not allow access to foreign objects that can cause bowel obstruction; do not feed dry diets exclusively; avoid heat.
Consult veterinarian; rehydrate; determine cause of dehydration and treat cause; remove from hot environment if applicable	Do not stress or handle pet more than necessary; do not give homemade salt and sugar mixtures that are not correctly balanced.
Veterinarian must trim teeth back to correct and even length; check teeth and trim them regularly throughout hamster's entire life	Do not use hamster in breeding program as malocclusion is often an inherited disorder
Contact veterinarian to determine cause; rehydrate immediately	Avoid group housing and stress; discontinue fruits and vegetables
Consult veterinarian to determine cause of problem	Do not handle more than necessary, especially around the head and ears

Dwarf Hamster Health Check Sheet (continued)

Health Problem	Symptoms	Causes
Eye problems	Clear or viscous discharge from eyes; closed eyes; eyes dull or cloudy	Infection; injury; irritating substances; disease
Gastrointestinal problems	Lack of appetite; weight loss; inactivity; pain; hunched-up position; constipation; lack of feces; diarrhea	Bacterial or viral infections; inadequate nutrition; parasites; change in diet; intestinal obstruction; unsanitary housing; stress
Heatstroke	Hot; weak; unresponsive; comatose; may appear to be dead	Exposure to high temperatures, heat sources, or sunlight; enclosure in hot environment; inadequate ventilation
Nails	Nails too long; may interfere with activities; may tear, bleed, and become infected	Reduced activity and wear of nails, or lack of rough surfaces to wear down nails
Rectal prolapse	Red, swollen, tube-shaped tissue protruding from anus; lack of appetite; lethargy	Inflamed, swollen intestines as a result of illness
Respiratory problems	Wheezing; sneezing; difficulty breathing; discharge from nose and eyes; lack of appetite; inactivity; weight loss	Viral, fungal, or bacterial infection; allergies; exposure to fine dusts; exposure to drafts or cold; damp environment
Scent gland infection (mid-ventral)	Swollen, reddened, sore, crusty, scabbed scent gland on belly	Irritation; poor or soiled housing conditions
Skin and fur problems	Loss of fur; sores; flaky or moist skin; redness; oozing; itching; scratching; infection	Bacterial or fungal infections; parasitism; improper diet; allergies; disease; hormonal imbalance
Trauma and broken bones	Inactivity; lack of appetite; inability to walk or sit normally; broken bones; bleeding; swelling; pain	Unlimited possibilities, including being dropped, stepped on, sat upon, trapped, and bitten

Do	Don't
Place hamster in a dark room; consult veterinarian for diagnosis	Avoid light, which can be painful to the injured eye; avoid stress and do not handle more than necessary
Isolate from other pets; rehydrate; contact veterinarian to determine cause of problem	Do not handle or stress more than necessary
Remove from heat; hold in hand and submerge body in cool water while keeping head above water; dry well and rehydrate as soon as pet is conscious	Do not handle or stress more than necessary; do not leave pet in hot area
Trim tips of nail with nail clippers designed for human babies	Do not trim close to base of nail or where a pink color can be seen through the nail
Contact your veterinarian; swollen tissue may be gently pushed back into anus or may need surgical correction	Do not wait to contact your veterinarian; a delay in treatment decreases the chances of survival
Contact your veterinarian; problem can quickly develop into pneumonia and result in death	Do not expose to cold or damp environment, or dusty cage material; do not handle or stress more than necessary
Soak and clean with gentle antiseptic solution	Do not squeeze gland or pick at scab
Contact your veterinarian for diagnosis and medication; keep skin and fur clean	Do not put drying products on dry skin, nor moisturizers on moist skin without first consulting a veterinarian
Observe closely to determine extent of injury; watch for normal behavior and movement; contact your veterinarian	Do not house with other animals; do not handle or stress any more than necessary

RAISING DWARF HAMSTERS

Raising dwarf hamsters is relatively easy (with the exception of the Chinese hamster), and it is also a lot of fun. You will encounter some challenges along the way, however, and there are some important facts you must know to be successful at your new hobby.

The most amazing aspect of hamster reproduction is the extremely short reproductive cycle. Of all the eutherian mammals (i.e., all mammals except egg-laying mammals and marsupials), the hamster has the most compressed reproductive cycle of any on this planet.

It makes sense when you think about it. A small animal that has several predators and a very short life span can ensure the survival of its species only by producing as many offspring as possible in its lifetime. Hamsters accomplish this in many ways:

1. They reach sexual maturity at a very early age.

2. They reproduce frequently.

3. Their gestation period (pregnancy) is very short.

4. They produce several young in each litter.

What is so amazing about the hamster's entire reproductive cycle is how short the time intervals are between these events.

Being able to correctly identify different species and color types is a necessary skill for successfully raising hamsters.

What does all this mean to you as a budding hamster breeder? For one thing, you need to pay close attention to your hamsters or you can suddenly end up with more than you planned! You will need to develop a scheduled breeding program so that you can control how many litters you produce. Before you breed your hamsters, make sure that you have definite homes lined up for the babies when they are ready to leave the nest.

The best way to be sure your hamsters do not breed without your permission is to separate the males from the females at the time of weaning. Most dwarf hamster siblings of the same sex can be housed together in peace, if you keep them together from weaning.

Each of the dwarf hamster species share similarities in their breeding behavior. They also have significant differences in their reproductive cycle and the manner in which they raise their young. First, we will consider the characteristics these animals share in common. Later, we will review each species and its particularities separately.

Reproductive Cycle

Hamsters are seasonal breeders—they breed only during a certain time of the year. Hamsters housed under controlled, artificial lighting conditions are the exception; they may breed year-round in captivity.

As a hamster breeder, you need to know your hamsters' breeding season so that you can optimize chances of producing a litter. If you have females that behave aggressively toward males, be sure to keep them separated, especially during the nonbreeding season.

Estrus

Estrus is the time during the breeding season that the female hamster will permit the male to mate with her. It is the time period just before and just after ovulation, when the female hamster's eggs are released from the ovaries.

In the hamster's rapid reproductive cycle, estrus lasts only about twelve hours. If a successful breeding takes place during estrus, the female becomes pregnant; otherwise, the female becomes aggressive toward the male and is not receptive to breeding until approximately three and one half to four days later, when she comes into estrus again. This four-day cycle will continue throughout the breeding season, unless the female becomes pregnant.

Breeding Behavior

During the breeding season, some hamsters may become aggressive. These individuals require direct supervision when placed with other animals in a cage. It is always best if you can be present to monitor your hamsters' activities. Be certain that your female hamster is actually willing to breed. If she is unreceptive and begins to attack the male hamster, remove her immediately. To be on the safe side, make sure the male has several hiding places where he can escape from the female if she becomes aggressive after mating.

The hamster's estrous cycle lasts four days, which means that every four days the non-pregnant female will accept the male for breeding. Estrus usually occurs shortly after the lights are turned off in the evening. This is the best time to observe whether your female hamster is willing to mate.

Hamster breeding techniques vary according to the species of hamster you own. For example, if Siberian hamsters are not housed

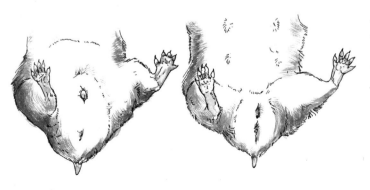

Male hamsters have a rounded bottom, due to the scrotum, and a greater anogenital distance than females. The sex of the baby hamsters can be determined by three weeks of age. Nipples are evident on the females and the urogenital distance is shorter than that of males.

together, it is difficult to know when the female is ready to breed. On the other hand, Djungarian hamster females that are housed separately from the male are easy to check for signs of willingness to breed by introducing the female into the male's cage. Chinese hamsters are not housed together all the time, or they will fight!

To be certain your female hamster is in estrus, place her in the male's cage. Always take the female to the male so that he will have the advantage of being in his own territory with his own scents. Sense of smell is a very important means of communication between hamsters. If the female is receptive, instead of aggressively attacking the male, she will sniff him and allow him to investigate her head, ears, and genital area. You do not have to wait long to see if your hamster is ready to breed. If the female is receptive, breeding will begin within fifteen minutes. If there is no sign of breeding within that time period, remove the female from the male's cage. If the female hamster begins to attack the male, remove her immediately. To avoid being bitten, use a can or jar to transfer the female out of the cage.

Lordosis

When the female is ready to accept the male, she makes ultrasonic noises to signal her interest. She then assumes a posture in which she braces her legs, holds her back flat, and lifts her tail. This position is called *lordosis*. The female may hold this position for a few minutes. It does not take long for the male hamster to attempt to mate. If he is young or inexperienced, he may first try to mount on the wrong end and grab the female's head, but in time he will figure out what to do. Some-

When the female is ready to breed, she will allow the male to approach her to sniff and investigate.

times the male moves the female around by grasping first one leg, then the other, until he finds a comfortable position. Even experienced males sometimes have difficulty mating if the female lifts her genital area too high or her tail is in the way. Eventually, the male will mount the female, breed, and dismount. The male may breed the female several times in a one-minute time period. The breeding activity can continue for up to an hour.

Keeping the Pair Together

It has been suggested that ejaculation, or the release of sperm, does not occur every time the male hamster mates. The matings in which ejaculation takes place appear to be characterized by the male holding his pelvis rigidly against the female for a few seconds. To be certain that a fertile breeding has occurred, keep your hamster pair together for at least two hours. If you are breeding Chinese hamsters, you may remove the female after two hours. Some breeders recommend leaving the female Chinese hamster with the male for up to six hours. If you are breeding *Phodopus* hamsters, leave the female with the male, but be sure he has enough space in which to hide in case she later becomes aggressive toward him. If you are raising Djungarian hamsters, it is especially important to keep the male and female together so that the female does not block the pregnancy (see Species-Specific Breeding Facts, page 91).

While your hamsters are together, watch them closely. Breeding takes a lot of energy and the male hamster may be exhausted by the time he is finished. If you are breeding Chinese hamsters, when you remove the male be sure to house him alone where he can rest in safety.

If the female becomes aggressive, the male will rebuff her by pushing her away with his front feet.

If you place him with other males, they may attack and injure him.

The Copulatory Plug

After a series of matings, a small, whitish-colored plug of waxy consistency may be seen on the female hamster's vaginal area. This is called a *copulatory plug* and it is normal. It is a good indicator that sperm were released during the breeding process.

Records

Be sure to record the date the breeding took place and mark the anticipated birth date on your calendar. You won't have long to wait. The pups will arrive before you know it!

Pregnancy

What exactly happens once a hamster becomes pregnant? Within one day of breeding, fertilization of the eggs, or ova, takes place. In less than four days, the fertilized eggs grow into embryos and move from the mother hamster's oviducts into her uterus. Another day passes and the embryos attach to the wall of the mother's uterus. This process is called *implantation;* it enables the embryos to develop into fetuses. Each fetus receives its nutrition for growth through its umbilical cord, which is connected to the placenta, an organ that joins the mother and the unborn offspring during pregnancy. Each placenta is implanted in the wall of the mother hamster's uterus.

The length of pregnancy, or gestation, varies for each species of dwarf hamster. The time period from conception, when the female becomes pregnant, to parturition, when she gives birth, can be eigtheen days or less.

Accelerated Reproduction

What is even more remarkable is that hamsters are able to become pregnant again on the same day they give birth! It is actually possible for a female hamster to mate, become pregnant, give birth, mate again, and give birth to a second litter, all within a thirty-six-day time frame. This is an amazing species survival mechanism, which makes it possible for hamsters to produce large numbers of babies in a short period of time.

This type of accelerated reproduction can make tremendous demands on a mother hamster. She must be able to lactate, providing milk for the newborn litter, and, at the same time, she must maintain good condition and eat enough so that the second litter can properly develop in her uterus. This is no small feat.

Implantation

What if times are too tough and it is too stressful for the mother hamster to carry a second litter while still nursing the first litter? Hamsters seem to have an answer for almost every survival-related situation. In this case, it is possible for the second litter to be held in a sort of suspended animation. This is done in one of two ways: One way is called *delayed implantation;* the other way is known as *postimplantation embryonic diapause,* and has been documented in Djungarian and Siberian hamsters. These phenomena explain why some hamsters appear to extend their length of pregnancy three to seven days longer than the usual gestation period.

In the case of delayed implantation, the development of the baby hamsters-to-be, which are still embryos, can be put on hold. The embryos do not attach to the wall of the mother's uterus eight days after conception, as they normally would; instead, the embryos attach nine or more days later.

Postimplantation embryonic diapause differs from delayed implantation in that the embryos have already attached to the wall of the mother's uterus; however, the development of the embryos is delayed a short time until conditions are more suitable for them to grow. Until the documentation of this adaptation, postimplantation embryonic diapause had only been observed in a few species of bats.

What determines whether implantation or embryonic development will be delayed in the dwarf hamster? We do not have all the answers, but researchers have learned a lot from the Djungarian and Siberian hamsters. In these species, if the existing litter is doing well and growing rapidly, the second litter is usually born after a normal gestation period. However, if the baby hamsters in the existing litter are small or not thriving, development of the unborn litter is delayed. This enables the mother hamster to focus all her energy and resources on nurturing the litter she already has in the nest.

Knowing If Breeding Took Place

Since *Phodopus* hamsters are often housed together, it is sometimes difficult to know when a breeding took place. If you check your female hamsters daily, you may see the copulatory plug (page 82). Female hamsters also have a thick, whitish vaginal discharge five days after breeding. This temporary discharge is normal and indicates the hamster is pregnant. If you do not see any of these signs, you may want to check whether your female is receptive to the male for breeding again. You can introduce her to the male four days after the first attempted breeding. If she is receptive and allows the male to breed, then she was not pregnant, but if she is unreceptive, remove her immediately. She may be pregnant and she might injure the male.

Behavior of the Pregnant Hamster

It can be difficult to tell if a hamster is pregnant just by looking at her. Her weight gain may be slight and her belly may not seem as large as you would expect, especially if she is carrying only a few pups. Your hamster's behavior will give you a good indication of her pregnancy status. Female hamsters become very aggressive and territorial as their delivery due date approaches. They spend a lot of their time building nests and chasing other hamsters away. She may turn her protective aggressions toward you, too, and try to bite, so watch your fingers!

Birth

Hamsters are very active all the way up to the time they give birth. A few hours before the pups are born, the mother hamster begins to breathe more rapidly than usual. She becomes restless and goes from one activity to the other: grooming, nest building, eating, and digging. At the onset of birth, she begins to clean her genital area. She sits up and crouches over to deliver her firstborn pup, which may be born headfirst or breech (tail first). She licks the pup clean of birth membranes and blood, and separates it from the placenta by chewing the umbilical cord. The mother then eats the placenta.

For many animal species, the placenta provides nutrition for the mother when she is nursing her young and is unable to leave them alone to search for food, but hamsters have everything planned in advance. They almost always have more food stored than they will ever be able to eat. *Phodopus* hamsters raise their young together, so the father can bring food to the nest. If the mother hamster does not eat the placenta when the pups are born, she diligently stores it in her food pile. If this happens, carefully remove the placentas before they start to rot and contaminate the cage.

Sometimes the pups are eaten along with the birth membranes and the placenta. Cannibalism is common and happens most frequently during the first week after birth, with hamsters that are first-time mothers, or that are nervous or upset. In order to avoid this catastrophe, the wriggling pups must attach themselves as quickly as possible to one of their mother's teats and begin suckling. Resist the temptation to handle the small, pink, hairless babies, as

The mother hamster sits up and crouches over to deliver her pups.

Born hairless, helpless and vulnerable, these babies, about the size of a dime, will be on their own in just 3 weeks.

this intrusion will upset the mother. She must be left completely alone; the slightest disturbance may cause her to eat or reject her pups.

Between births, the mother hamster resumes her various activities: scurrying about the cage digging, grooming, and working on her nests. If she is housed with other hamsters, she will chase them from her pups and her nest areas. The mother hamster may give birth to her pups in different areas of the cage, but she will eventually gather them up and place them all together in a nest.

It does not take long for the mother hamster to have her babies. The entire process is usually completed within a few minutes. When she has finished, she will stretch and arch her back over the pups, while supporting herself on rigid legs. This is called *huddling.* It is the mother's way of covering her pups without crushing them. By huddling, she can keep her babies warm while they eat and sleep.

Maternal Care

An important first step in maternal care is nest building. The mother hamster is already making arrangements and preparing to care for her young. Although all hamsters build nests, pregnant hamsters usually are more creative and build more elaborate nests; in fact, there seems to be a correlation between good nest building and pup survival. Often, hamsters that have built small, sloppy nests do not successfully raise many of their babies. On the other hand, hamsters that are meticulous nest builders are usually attentive parents.

Warmth: Since the pups are born naked and helpless, they are totally dependent upon their mother for warmth and food. They are unable to thermoregulate, or maintain body warmth, on their own. They need their mother to huddle over them and keep them warm until their fur grows and they are able to control their body temperature on their own.

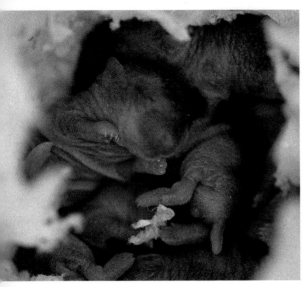

The best mother hamsters build the best nests. Here's a rare peek inside one of them.

Dwarf hamsters have adapted to very cold weather in their native habitat, but even in the wild, the pups are kept in a warm environment. The air inside the hamster's underground burrows is usually around room temperature.

Lactation, or milk production by the mother (see page 87), requires energy. The mother hamster has to eat and drink more than usual to produce milk. Her metabolism increases when she produces milk and she generates heat. The heat from the mother's body keeps the pups warm, and when the babies suckle, she generates even more body heat. When the pups are naked, they absorb more heat from the mother than they do when they have fur. As the pups grow fur, they become less dependent on their mother for heat. Instead of absorbing heat from her body, they eventually maintain and create body warmth themselves.

It is possible for the mother hamster to become too hot as she tends to all of her duties, so she has to leave her pups once in a while so that she can cool down. When the mother leaves the nest, she covers her pups completely with nesting material to keep them warm and well hidden until she returns. She usually keeps some food within reach of the nest.

Litters in a colony: When *Phodopus* hamsters live together peacefully in a colony, females sometimes give birth to litters on or about the same day. The mothers may share their duties, moving pups from one nest to the other and nursing each other's babies. This is just another one of the hamster's many ways of ensuring survival of its species. If the mother of a litter of pups should die, another mother might adopt the pups and add them to her family, but this is not always the case. Mother hamsters are very protective of their young. They can behave fiercely toward any intruders, including members of their own species. If your hamsters are housed in groups, be sure they are all compatible. Do not add new hamsters to the established colony. Remove any hamsters that insist on fighting. For the safety of the litter, and to avoid being bitten, resist the temptation to handle the pups during their first two weeks of life.

Paternal Care

The father hamster is a prominent figure in *Phodopus* family circles and he plays an important part in raising the pups. Although the mother may chase him from the nest the day the pups are born, within one or two days she will welcome him back to help her with the babies.

Of the three *Phodopus* species, the Djungarian hamster father plays the most important role. Male pheromones stimulate hormonal secretion in the female and ensure continuity of her reproductive cycle. If the male is removed from the female within two days after mating, his pheromones are no longer present to stimulate continuation of the pregnancy. The absence of pheromones signals the female that the male will not be available in the future to help her raise the pups. At this point in time, the pregnancy can be blocked from continuing, so great is the female's dependence upon the male to help raise the pups.

When the mother Djungarian hamster becomes too hot and needs to leave the nest to cool down, it is the father that huddles the pups. When the mother hamster is nursing the pups and cannot leave the nest, it is the father that brings her meals. And when the pups start to crawl about and wander from the nest, it is often the father that retrieves them and brings them back home. Laboratory studies have shown that when the Djungarian hamster father is not present to help raise the pups, their survival is greatly reduced. The need for the father's continued presence is greater in the wild than in captivity. Pet hamsters do not have to leave the nest for long periods of time and travel great distances in cold weather to search for food, so the naked pups have less chance of dying of cold.

Although both species are adapted for life in cold weather, the Siberian hamster can tolerate heat and extreme cold better than the Djugarian hamster. This is an important difference in adaptability between these two closely related species. It explains why it is possible for Siberian hamster mothers to successfully raise

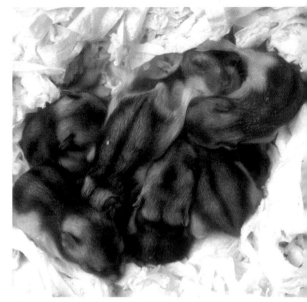

By nine days of age, the babies are fully furred, but still have a lot of growing to do!

their pups without the help of the father, if necessary.

Lactation

Lactation is the production of milk by the mammary glands, or breasts. The composition of milk—its percentage of fat, protein, and water—varies for each species. Lactation is a unique feature of all mammals. It makes it possible for mother animals to nourish their immature young safely in hiding, any time, anywhere. It is a practical approach to increase survival of offspring during times of food shortage.

When a mother is lactating, she is turning the food she has eaten and the fat she has stored into milk for her babies. This process requires energy and burns up calories. It makes

Baby hamsters open their eyes by 10 days of age.

it necessary for the mother to eat more food and drink more water than usual.

The body heat hamsters produce when they lactate keeps the pups warm. Mother hamsters may lose weight during lactation, so be sure to provide lots of nutritious food and plenty of water during that time. Since the mother may not want to leave the nest, you can supplement her moisture intake by providing small pieces of fresh apple.

Sexing Baby Hamsters

It is not difficult to determine the sex of the baby hamsters at an early age. Although you will not be handling the pups until they are two weeks old, you may have an opportunity to see their little bellies as they writhe about in their nest. The teats of the females are usually visible by eight days of age.

When the hamsters are three weeks old and ready to be weaned, you can handle them safely and have a good look. Hold the baby carefully, belly up, with its back against the palm of your hand. You may hold the tail gently, but do not pull on it. Once you have identified the anus, located under the tail, proceed upward to the genital opening. The distance between the anus and the urethral orifice, or the anogenital distance, is greater in males than in females. The males have a more rounded posterior because of the presence of the scrotum, while the females' posterior is more pointed and two rows of teats are visible on the belly.

Weaning

A weaned animal is an animal that no longer requires and is no longer receiving nourishment from its mother's milk. Baby hamsters may begin nibbling solid food as early as ten days of age, but they still need their mother's milk to survive. They will also start to explore their surroundings when their eyes and ears open and they are able to walk. During this time you can help them along by providing tiny pieces of apple. They will benefit from the added moisture, especially if they are still too small to use the water bottle. The pups will depend on their mother for complete nutrition until they are eighteen to twenty-one days old. At that time you can remove them from their mother and house the siblings together in same-sex groups. Do not put the pups in with adult hamsters that can injure them.

Imprinting and Taming

Imprinting is what takes place when a very young animal sees another animal and immediately forms a close bond with it. In nature, baby animals almost always imprint on their mothers. She is the first thing they see, smell, hear, and recognize. They depend on her for protection. They follow her and learn from her. The same is true for hamsters. By the time you are able to handle the pups without threatening their safety, they already will have imprinted on their mother.

This in no way interferes with your ability to tame your baby hamster. Regular handling soon after weaning will make it a gentle and responsive pet. It will quickly recognize you as a friend and provider of food and look forward to your visits.

Raising the Babies

One of the most important things you can do for your baby hamsters is to be sure they always have enough to drink. Be sure the sipper tube of the water bottle is within their reach. Leave them small pieces of apple for added moisture.

Your baby hamsters can be housed just like the adults. They have the same needs: nutritious food, comfortable temperature, and safe, escape-proof housing.

Of course, handling the pups will be a challenge because they are so small, but regular handling is an important part of keeping your pets tame and friendly. If you cup your hand around them carefully, and handle them gently, they will be a joy to hold.

The Babies Leave Home

As tempting as it is, you probably will not keep every baby hamster you raise. By this time you have gained quite a bit of experience in hamster habits and care. As a responsible ham-

The pups have arrived and now you have a handful!

ster breeder, you will be sure that the pups are going to loving homes where they will receive good care.

To be sure everything goes well for the pups, provide the new owners with as much information as you can about their care. Show them the type of cage you use to house your hamsters. Demonstrate how to pick up the pups and examine them. Give the new owners a bag of the food you are currently feeding. This will prevent the stress of a change in diet. Finally, in case of a problem, recommend any veterinarians you know who have a special interest in pocket pets.

At one week of age, this baby dwarf hamster is almost as long as a matchstick.

SPECIES-SPECIFIC BREEDING FACTS

Each species of dwarf hamster differs in its reproductive characteristics, breeding season, response to environmental influences, and the way it raises its family. These species-specific traits play an important role as you decide which species to raise, how many hamsters to keep, how much space you can give them, which breeding methods to use, and the amount of time you can dedicate to raising hamsters.

The Djungarian Hamster

The breeding season for the Djungarian hamster is from April through September. Since Djungarian hamsters will mate and conceive the same day a litter is born, they are capable of producing and weaning a litter every eighteen days; however, litters are usually produced every nineteen days. Gestation varies from eighteen to twenty days, due to the hamster's ability to delay implantation or delay development of the embryos. Some pregnancies can be developmentally delayed three to seven days. These delays are determined by how rapidly the pups in the existing litter are growing. If they are not growing as much as they should, or if they need special attention from the mother, the birth of the subsequent litter is delayed. The average litter size is eight pups.

Phodopus hamsters form close bonds with their mates.

Djungarian hamsters are very sensitive to their environment. An increase in temperature, a reduction in water availability, or shortened daylight periods all cause a drop in the hamster's fertility. They may also increase the gestation period.

The Family Unit

Djungarian hamsters prefer to form monogamous bonds. By keeping the same mate, there is no upset in the family unit, which relies heavily on the father hamster.

Djungarian hamsters are biparental, meaning both parents are *necessary* for survival of the babies. Before their first litter is born, male Djungarian hamsters undergo hormonal changes that researchers believe stimulate their strong paternal (fatherly) behavior. The male also secretes pheromones that affect the female hamster's physiology and that are necessary for her to maintain her pregnancy.

When the pups are born, the Djungarian hamster male assists in the birth process by licking away amniotic fluid and clearing away fetal membranes so the pups can breathe. The males have even been observed to eat the placentas. Father Djungarian hamsters also help raise the pups by keeping them warm when the mother leaves the nest and by bringing food to the family in the nest.

Studies showed that in Djungarian hamster families where the father hamster was present, pup survival was approximately 95 percent; in families where the father was absent, pup survival dropped to 47 percent.

Temperature

Ambient temperature is another factor critical to pup survival. Djungarian hamsters can adapt to the cold environment they inhabit in the wild, but in captivity they do not tolerate heat or cold as well as other dwarf hamsters. Their pups are especially sensitive to the cold, and until they are fully furred and able to thermoregulate, the youngsters depend on their parents for body heat. A drop in ambient

temperature from approximately room temperature to a few degrees above freezing can reduce pup survival to 32 percent.

Sense of Smell

Like all hamsters, the Djungarian hamster's sense of smell is very keen. The presence, or absence, of specific odors strongly influences its reproductive cycle. For example, if the male hamster is removed from the female's presence within two days of mating, there are no scents indicating a male presence. The female may interpret this to mean that the male may not be available to help raise the litter-to-be, in which case she can block, or prevent, implantation of the embryos from taking place. When this happens, the litter that would have resulted from the breeding never develops or comes to term.

Interbreeding

Although it is possible for Djungarian and Siberian hamsters to interbreed in a laboratory setting, this is not a usual occurrence because they are different species. They recognize their differences and tend to fight with each other. In the event of a mating and pregnancy, the resulting hybrid offspring usually are infertile or have reduced fertility and rarely reproduce. Djungarian hamsters will not breed with Roborovskii or Chinese hamsters.

The Siberian Hamster

The breeding season for the Siberian hamster is from April through September. Siberian hamsters are dedicated to their mates and form close monogamous bonds. During their partnership, the hamsters live in harmony, mate

No wonder hamster breeders rise to the challenge of raising Chinese hamsters. No matter which coloration you prefer, you have to admit, they're cute. Dominant spot on the left, wild type on the right.

several times, build nests, and raise their litters together.

Siberian hamsters are uniparental. This means that unlike Djungarian hamsters, the presence and assistance of the male Siberian hamster is not essential to the survival of the litter. He may help the mother raise the pups, but she can also manage without him. Siberian hamsters do not show all of the same strong paternal behaviors as Djungarian hamsters. Species differences, as well as differences in metabolism and thermoregulation seem to account for this fact. So it comes as no surprise that Siberian hamsters very rarely mate with Djungarian hamsters and when they do, it is under unnatural conditions. Any pups resulting from such a mating are hybrids. The female hybrids have reduced fertility and the male hybrids are infertile (sterile). This is due to an abnormal pairing of the X and Y chromosomes during meiosis.

Siberian hamsters will not mate with Desert or Chinese hamsters. They breed and bond with members of their own species, plain and simple.

The bond between the male and female Siberian hamster pair is so strong that if the animals are separated, their behavior changes. The males become inactive, eat more food, and show behavioral changes similar to some types of depression in humans. The hamster's depression is accompanied by an increase in weight, and even obesity. Many of the male's hormone

levels change so that the testicles decrease in size. So striking are these changes that researchers study Siberian hamsters to learn more about depression, hormone changes, and obesity.

Effect of the Environment

The Siberian hamster is very sensitive to its environment. Any change in ambient temperature, photoperiod, and water availability can affect its reproductive cycle dramatically. In fact, as winter approaches and the days shorten, there is an entire collapse of the Siberian hamster's reproductive capacities. The females do not come into estrus and the males' testicles shrink to one tenth of breeding season size. They become less active, sleep more, and their body temperature drops. Under the right temperature and light conditions, Siberian hamsters may enter a state of torpor. Even their fur changes color, turning from gray to white. When the days become longer, the breeding cycle begins again.

Recent Reproductive Studies in Siberian Hamsters

Recent studies show that during the short day cycles (winter months) the Siberian ham-

ster's testes shrink drastically in size, and so testosterone production also drops dramatically. Interestingly, during short day cycles, Siberian hamsters on study were observed to become more aggressive. The studies concluded that the increased aggression in male Siberian hamsters was directly related to the reduction in the photoperiod (hours of exposure to daylight).

Another study suggests that sex hormones play an important role in the Siberian hamster's immune function and that an increase in sex hormones increases the hamster's immunity. From this study, pet owners can surmise that their Siberian hamsters may be more likely to become ill in the winter months if they are housed under conditions (short photoperiod and low temperatures) that lead to a drop in sex hormone production, which in turn can lower the animal's immunity.

Siberian hamsters are social animals, but social interactions can be very stressful for them, as was recently proven in a complex research project. Cortisol is a hormone released by the body under stress. Cortisol generally suppresses immunity, so stressed animals are more prone to infections and health problems. The study showed that Siberian hamster pairs that include at least one male (two males or a male and female) have higher levels of social stress interactions than two females housed together. The pairs with males had higher cortisol levels than the female/female pair. So, if you are not breeding your female Siberian hamsters, consider housing them in female/female pairs to reduce social stress.

The Desert Hamster

The breeding season for the Desert hamster, *Phodopus roborovskii*, spans from April through September. The gestation period is twenty to twenty-two days. A single female hamster may produce as many as four litters during the breeding season. The length of gestation for each subsequent litter is often shorter than the length of gestation of the preceding litter. In other words, the mother may carry her first litter twenty-two days before the pups are born, yet carry the second litter only twenty-one days, and the third litter twenty days. Litter size ranges from one to nine, and averages three to six pups.

Desert hamsters will not breed with Djungarian, Siberian, or Chinese hamsters.

The Chinese Hamster

Light Cycles and Environment

Chinese hamsters are not easy to raise in captivity. The two most important elements for successfully raising Chinese hamsters are controlled light cycles (twelve hours of light followed by twelve hours of darkness) and a very quiet environment. Females come into estrus shortly after the dark period begins. Males will breed and form copulatory plugs only one to two hours after the dark period begins. During the dark period, no light, not even for an instant, should enter the breeding room because it will disrupt the hamsters' reproductive cycle.

How do you prevent light from coming in when you enter a room to check on your hamsters? And how can you observe them in the dark to see if they have mated? To successfully raise Chinese hamsters, you need a special housing setup, and equipment similar to those used in research laboratories, including red light illumination. You also must keep noise to an absolute minimum during breeding and pregnancy, and when raising the pups. Chinese hamsters are very sensitive to noise and will not reproduce or raise their young if they are disturbed. Finally, room temperature should be between 72°F to 74°F (22°C to 23.3°C) with a relative humidity of approximately 50 percent.

As you can see, if you are going to accept the challenge of raising Chinese hamsters, you must be dedicated from the onset. Your local pet store or hamster club can put you in touch with Chinese hamster suppliers from whom you can purchase your breeding stock and obtain additional information. Also, some universities raise Chinese hamsters; the college or university nearest you may be able to put you in contact with a university that maintains Chinese hamster colonies. Universities can share with you the breeding techniques that work best for them.

General Facts About Breeding Chinese Hamsters

Start with the best breeding stock you can obtain. If possible, buy males less than fifteen months of age that are experienced breeders and that have already produced litters. Try to buy females less than one year of age that are nonaggressive. This is easier said than done. Female Chinese hamsters can treat males

Dwarf Hamster Reproduction

	P. campbelli	P. roborovskii	P. sungorus	C. griseus
Breeding season	April to September	April to September	April to September	February to October
Level of difficulty	Easy to raise in captivity	Easy to raise in captivity	Easy to raise in captivity	Difficult to raise in captivity
Gestation	18 to 22 days	20 to 22 days	18 to 25 days	21 days
Litter size	8 pups	6 pups	4 to 6 pups	4 pups
Litters/year	3 to 4	3 to 4	3 to 4	2 to 3
Father helps raise pups	Yes; biparental	Yes; uniparental	Yes; uniparental	No; uniparental
Weight at birth	.05 ounce (1.5 g)	.04 to .07 ounce (1 to 2 g)	.06 ounce (1.8 g)	.07 to 0.1 ounce (2 to 3 g)
Teeth and claws	Birth	Birth	Birth	Birth
Whiskers	3 days	3 days	3 days	3 days
Skin pigments	4 days	4 days	4 days	4 days
Body hair	6 days	5 days	6 days	7 days
Eyes/ears open	9 days	14 days	10 days	14 days
Weaned	21 days	19 days	20 days	21 days
Sexual maturity	2 months	4½ months	1½ to 2 months	3 months

so badly that some universities have resorted to breeding Chinese hamsters by artificial insemination.

Sometimes, sibling males and females can be raised together from the time of weaning. If they are compatible, they may breed when they become sexually mature. Another method that has resulted in litters is to place three males in a very large cage with three to five female littermates. Unfortunately, these techniques are not without risk and males are often killed by each other or the females.

In order for male Chinese hamsters to remain sexually active, they must have a female to breed two to three times each week. If you are raising Chinese hamsters, you will need to keep a lot of females available in order to maintain your male hamster's fertility level.

Female Chinese hamsters differ from *Phodopus* hamsters in that it is possible to examine them to know if they are ready to breed. If the female is in estrus, the genital area will be pink and swollen. Since hamsters usually come into estrus shortly after the lights are turned off, you should examine the female about one hour later, during the dark period. If the female appears ready to breed, place her in the male's cage. If she does not fight with the male, leave her with him for six hours. Before returning

the female to her own cage, check her genital area for evidence of a copulatory plug. Sometimes these can fall out and become lost in the bedding material. If you are not sure whether a mating took place, you can place the female in the male's cage four days later—be sure to stay right there to observe. If the female is already pregnant, she will treat the male viciously and you will need to remove her immediately.

Detecting Pregnancy

Although pregnancy is not always easy to detect in *Phodopus* hamsters, it can be detected in the Chinese hamster. If you are very observant, you may see a small spot of blood on the female's genital area fifteen days after breeding took place. This is normal and indicates the hamster is pregnant. Pups are born after a twenty-one-day gestation period. Females return to estrus the day after the pups are born. If the litter dies, the female will return to estrus within a few days and breed again.

The Pups

Cannibalism is common among Chinese hamsters. It can be reduced by making sure the room is quiet, by not disturbing the mother, and by supplementing her diet with wheat germ and a fresh slice of apple daily.

Chinese hamsters do not easily reproduce in captivity. Dominant spot on the left, wild type on the right.

If you have several females with pups born the same day, you can sometimes foster some pups from a large litter to a different mother with a smaller litter. Fostering is also useful if a mother becomes ill or dies. Pups should be fostered when they are three to four days old. Chinese hamster mothers will usually reject fostered pups older than four days.

Breeding Methods

Hamsters can be bred using a variety of methods; not every method is right for each species. Now that you have the information you need about your hamster's special reproductive requirements, you can decide which of these methods will work best for you.

Hand-Mating Method

This is a simple method. Soon after you have turned out the lights for the evening, place the female hamster in the male's cage. Within fifteen minutes, if the female is in estrus, she will assume the position of lordosis and breeding will take place. If she is not receptive to the male, she may become aggressive and attack him. Remove the female immediately and try again the next day. This method does not always work for Siberian hamsters.

Breeding Pair Method

This method has the advantage of saving time because the male and the female are always housed together. When they are ready, they will breed. The disadvantage of this method is that you usually will not know when a breeding takes place, so you will not know when the pups are due. Since Djungarian and Siberian hamsters form monogamous pairs, this technique works well for them. It is not recommended for Chinese hamsters because of their aggressive nature.

Harem Method

The harem method gives one male access to several females. There are three major advantages of this method: It saves time because you do not have to check females for estrus or compatibility; females are not overcrowded, so they do not stop their reproductive cycles; and the male can escape safely from the females, if necessary. The major disadvantage is that this technique requires special caging and collar equipment. You also may not know when matings occurred or when pups are due.

To use the harem method, several females and one male are housed separately in individual cages. A plastic tunnel connects the male's cage to each of the females' cages. The male is free to run from his cage through the tunnel

and into any of the females' cages. Each female is fitted with a special collar that stands out from her neck like a small satellite dish. The collar makes it impossible for the females to leave their cages or fit through the tunnel. If any of the females are nonreceptive and aggressive, the male can escape from them.

The harem method works well for raising Chinese hamsters. It is not recommended for *Phodopus* species, because the father participates in rearing the pups and monogamous pair bonds are formed.

Hybrids

Rarely, two closely related species may interbreed and produce offspring. These offspring are not members of either of their parents' species. They are hybrids, a type of animal that shares the genetics of two species but belongs to none. Hybrids are rare in nature and usually cannot reproduce.

Although different dwarf hamster species may closely resemble each other, they are distinctly different in their biology, genetic makeup, and social behavior. For this reason, most dwarf hamsters cannot interbreed, and those that can usually will not. Among the hamsters discussed here, only the Djungarian and Siberian hamsters can interbreed, an unusual occurrence that takes place only in captivity. In fact, attempts to breed a Siberian male to a Djungarian female have resulted in the male killing the female.

Some breeders are concerned that producing dwarf hamster hybrids will diminish the purity of the hamster type. In reality, the breeding for hybrids is not commonplace, and of the small number of hamster hybrids produced, female hybrids have reduced fertility, and male hybrids are sterile. This infertility is due to a mismatch of genetic material at the onset of development.

Hybrids may be difficult to tell apart from a true species. If you are planning on raising hamsters, be sure the hamsters you purchase are not hybrids, and buy from a reputable supplier.

BREEDING FOR COAT COLORS AND TEXTURES

Breeding for coat colors and textures is fun and educational. To be successful, a hamster breeder must start with top quality, healthy animals that are carriers of the desired color genes. The breeder must also have an excellent understanding of genetics and coat color inheritance, strong math skills, and keep accurate breeding records.

One of the most exciting aspects of raising dwarf hamsters is discovering the various types of color combinations that can be created through selective breeding. With solid knowledge of genetic inheritance, and color genetics, and some perseverance, you can produce some very fancy hamsters. To achieve the color results you want, you must first start out with animals that are already carrying the genes for the specific colors and patterns you wish to produce. You will have more colors to choose from when you buy directly from a hamster breeder, especially one that exhibits fancy hamsters and is active in hamster clubs and shows.

If you wish to produce colors and patterns, you will probably limit your species selection to the Djungarian and Siberian hamsters. The Desert hamster's colors range from shades of brown, to sandy, to apricot. So far it does not have the variety of colors seen in the other *Phodopus* hamsters. The Chinese hamster appears set in its gray to gray–brown coloration embellished with white markings in animals that carry the gene for dominant spot. Also, for reasons previously discussed, the Chinese hamster is difficult to raise in captivity.

Color Genetics

Genetics and coat color inheritance are complicated topics. Indeed, there are many books available that contain detailed information on these subjects (see Additional Reading, page 108). We will review the basics and describe some of the hamster colors currently recognized.

Fur and eye color are determined by the hamster's genetic makeup. Half of a hamster's genetic material comes from its father, the other half from its mother. For each hamster trait, there are at least two genes, one inherited from each parent, that determine what the hamster will be like. Often, several genes are responsible for a specific trait. The genes interact in such a way that characteristics may or may not be observed in the individual hamster, yet may be present in its genetic makeup, able to be passed on to future generations.

Depending on how genes for particular traits are expressed, they are called *dominant, codominant, recessive,* or *sex-linked* (traits that are genetically linked to the animal's sex and X chromosome). Dominant genes override the observable effects of recessive genes. Recessive gene traits are not evident unless the hamster has received the gene for the recessive trait from each of its parents. Codominant genes produce effects that fall somewhere in between what you would expect from a dominant or recessive gene.

Let's say you want to produce a pup of a certain color and that this color in controlled by only two genes. If the desired color is inherited in a dominant fashion, only one parent needs to be carrying the gene for that specific color for you to have a good chance of producing some pups of that color. However, if the color you wish to produce is inherited in a recessive fashion, both parents must be carrying the gene in order to produce some pups of the desired color. A parent can be carrying the recessive gene for the color, without actually being that color. This explains why sometimes you will find pups in a litter that are not the same color as either parent. It is likely the parents were each carrying a recessive gene for the pups' color.

Fortunately for the color genetics enthusiast who enjoys a challenge, the inheritance of coat color is much more complicated. Color is often determined by the interaction of several genes. The genes that control eye color may or may not be linked to the genes responsible for coat color. Before you know it, you are creating Punnett squares to figure out the different color possibilities your breeding animals might produce. You're not alone! For this purpose, known color genes have been assigned letters, with capital letters representing dominant genes and small letters representing recessive genes. For example, the gene that codes for albinism is called c, and is written as a small letter because albinism is a recessive trait.

To complicate matters, genes will sometime mutate, or change. Many, if not most, mutations in nature have harmful, rather than beneficial, effects. Sometimes gene mutations result in new colors and patterns. Sometimes these color and pattern mutations also cause health problems or deformities.

Today, several color varieties of hamsters have resulted from combining animals of the basic colors listed, and no doubt the list will grow. Maybe you will be one of the breeders to produce a new and unusual healthy color variation in your own line of dwarf hamsters.

The Djungarian Hamster

Coat Colors

The Djungarian hamster may be found in many colors, from the brownish-gray wild-type coloration, to blue-gray, lilac, champagne, light fawn, beige, and dark chocolate.

Agouti wild type: The Djungarian hamster is usually brownish gray, or a grizzled brown with black-tipped hairs, known as *agouti*. It has a dark dorsal stripe and an ivory-colored belly. The eyes are black. This basic color pattern is called the *wild type*. The wild type gene is

Dwarf hamsters have a keen sense of smell and mark their territories with their scent glands.

dominant. Most other coat colors observed in the Djungarian hamster are caused by the interaction of recessive genes.

Albino: Albinism, a complete lack of body and hair pigmentation, is found in many animal species. The coat is white and the eyes are pink or red. It is a recessive condition.

Pink-eyed dilution mutant: This hamster is not an albino. Although the eyes are not pigmented, and are pink or red, the rest of the animal is colored. The pink-eyed dilution mutant's color ranges from sandy yellow to deep apricot to light reddish orange. The undercoat is gray and the belly is ivory. The dorsal stripe varies from gray to buff, the ears are pink, and the eyes are red. Hamster breeders refer to this animal as an *argenté*. Argenté

comes from the French word, meaning "silvery."

There are two main types in cinnamon color:

1. Natural yellow red eye

2. Natural yellow black eye

These hamsters are cinnamon colored with gray base color, cream-colored belly, and a gray dorsal stripe. The red-eyed animals are generally lighter in color than black-eyed animals. Genetic inheritance for the eye color is separate from that for coat color but may be linked. Argenté mottled colors and patterns can be created by breeding an argenté hamster to a mottled hamster.

Black-eyed argenté: This hamster's color is sandy apricot to light orange with gray ears. Its eyes are black. Although it is called an argenté, it is not a pink-eyed dilution mutant.

Black: This hamster is black with a dark, or black belly, and may have a small amount of white on the throat. It has a barely perceptible black dorsal stripe and black eyes.

Dark sable: The dark sable hamster is a very dark chocolate color, also called *sable* or *black*, even though it is not a true black. The dorsal stripe is black and difficult to see against the dark coat. The eyes are black.

Dove: This hamster is a light sandy-gray with a brown dorsal stripe and red eyes. It may be a variation of the D dilution gene in the autosomal recessive homozygous form, *dd*. This hamster can be produced by breeding an argenté hamster to a black hamster.

White: This hamster is white, but it may have a few pigmented hairs in small areas or patches. Eyes are black.

Opal: The opal hamster has a silvery blue coat, cream to ivory belly, gray ears, and black eyes. The dorsal stripe is gray.

White color patterns: In addition to the various coat colors previously discussed, the amount of white that can appear in the Djungarian hamster's coat may also vary. The genes responsible for the white patterns, called *ticking* and *mottling,* are different from the ones that produce solid white coats. They are also different from the gene that causes albinism. In fact, it appears that the genes responsible for the two types of mottling patterns are even different from each other.

Platinum: Some hamsters have hundreds of white hairs distributed evenly throughout the coat. This makes the coat color appear lighter or paler than the base color. This overall lighter impression is called *platinum*. Platinum hamsters occur in all colors, including cinnamon, light brown, and black. Platinum hamsters can be produced by breeding a platinum hamster to a nonplatinum hamster.

Mottled: The mottled Djungarian hamster has white areas distributed throughout its coat. The hamster may seem to be mostly white with colored spots, or mostly colored with white spots. The head remains colored. The white mottling pattern is random and no two animals are exactly alike; however, the gene for mottling behaves in a codominant manner. Any hamster that carries the gene has a mottled coat pattern. Mottled pups can be produced only if at least one parent is mottled. If the mottled parent is mostly colored, with white spots, about one fourth of its offspring will have similar markings. If the mottled parent is mostly white, with colored spots, all its offspring will be mottled, but have much less white than the parent. If both parents are mottled, there will be a greater number of mottled pups in the litter, including some pups that are almost all white. If both parents are mottled almost all white, then all their pups will be almost entirely white.

Ruby-eyed mottled: This is a different gene from the mottled coat pattern gene, but it also behaves in a codominant manner. The white color pattern is different from that observed in the mottled hamster. The white markings are limited to the area around the neck, forming a white collar, and a few white spots on the back. A significant difference is the presence of red eyes in the ruby-eyed mottled Djungarian hamster.

While the ruby-eyed mottled hamster is an attractive addition to the breeding colony, you should avoid breeding two ruby-eyed mottled hamsters together. The pups that inherit the ruby-eyed mottled gene from each parent are born with several abnormalities, including being undersized, having undeveloped eyes,

and missing front teeth. These pups can be identified by their all-white color and their tiny size. They usually die within three weeks of birth.

White-Bellied hamster, also known as the Anophthalmic white: This hamster has a pure white abdomen. The rest of the body may be any color, but usually the back is sprinkled with white hairs and often a small white patch is present. Eyes are usually pink. They reflect a ruby color when light is shined directly on them. Do not breed two White-Bellied hamsters together. They will produce offspring that are anophthalmic (do not have eyes), or that have tiny, pink, malformed eyes and are blind.

Coat Textures

The Djungarian hamster normally has a smooth, even coat; however, variations in coat textures exist. By breeding animals with these variations, hamster breeders have established genetic lines with coat textures different from that found in the wild. These coat textures,

which are recessive to the wild type, add another element to the fun of raising dwarf hamsters.

Satin coat: The satin coat is not sleek and glossy as the name would suggest; rather, it appears wet or oily. Satin hamsters that are light-colored or white tend to have a yellow hue to their coat, making them look less clean than they are. The yellow coloration becomes more noticeable as the hamsters age. Satin hamsters exist in many colors. The satin coat is recessive to the normal coat, so both parents must be carrying the satin gene to produce offspring with satin coats.

Wavy coat: The wavy coat is a temporary condition. The fur is wavy and the whiskers are curly when the hamster is young. As the hamster ages and sheds, a normal coat grows in its place. The whiskers remain curled.

Rex coat: Rex-coat type has been reported in Djungarian hamsters, but this may be an uncommon variation of the wavy coat. The rex coat is thin, soft, fuzzy, and tightly curled and the whiskers are curly.

Hamster "jewels": the Siberian Pearl is white with some black or purple-gray hairs on its head.

Whiskers: Curly whiskers may be an interesting feature in hamster appearance, but curly whiskers are certainly less useful than straight whiskers. Since the hamster has poor eyesight and relies heavily on its whiskers for navigation, one questions the merit of promoting this trait.

The Siberian Hamster

The Siberian hamster occurs in three basic colors: dark gray, lilac–blue, or purple–gray, and predominantly white with a colored head. Remember that another name for the Siberian hamster is the Winter White Russian hamster. This name comes from the fact that no matter what color the Siberian hamster is, it may still turn white in the winter in response to a decrease in daylight hours and a drop in temperature.

Colors

Agouti wild type: The most common color of the Siberian hamster, and the color found in the wild, is dark gray with a black dorsal stripe, a white belly, and black eyes.

Sapphire: The sapphire Siberian hamster is a blue–gray or purple–gray color with a dark gray dorsal stripe, an ivory belly, and black eyes. It is also known as the blue natural.

Pearl: The body of the pearl Siberian hamster is almost all white, with gray or black hairs scattered sparsely through the coat. The head and spine are mostly colored. Where colored hair is present on the back, areas of the dorsal stripe can be observed.

Pearl Sapphire: The Pearl Sapphire has lighter ticking coloration and lighter ear coloration than the Pearl.

The Chinese Hamster

Colors

Wild type: In the wild, the
Chinese hamster is gray–brown with
a light gray to ivory-colored belly,
a dark brown or black dorsal stripe,
and black eyes. This is also the most
common color of pet Chinese hamsters.

Dominant spot: Some Chinese hamsters
have the gene that codes for splashes of white
markings on the coat. These hamsters are
almost all white, with colored spots or patches
all over the body.

Reports of a new color, the "black-eyed
white" Chinese hamster, are actually cases of
mistaken identity. The "black-eyed white" is
genetically nothing more than a Dominant spot
hamster with extreme white-spotting. It is not
a new color mutation.

*The dominant spot pattern is a color
mutation of Chinese hamsters. The hamster
has patches of white on its body. Some
patches can be so large the animal is
almost all white.*

Exhibiting Dwarf Hamsters

Now that you have spent time learning about
hamsters and raising some beautiful litters, you
want to show off your accomplishments. What
could be better than a hamster show?

Hamster shows are usually hosted by hamster clubs. You can learn from various sources
where a hamster show is going to be held. Your
local pet store can put you in touch with other
hamster breeders and hamster club officials
who will know what events are going to take
place. Many pet magazines, available at your
pet shop or in book stores, are full of information about animal shows. You can also contact
the supervisor of your local fairgrounds to
inquire about animal-related activities that
take place there. Your veterinarian is also a

good source of information for local clubs,
associations, and exhibits, and of course you
can use the Internet to locate hamster breeders
and web sites.

Once you learn of an upcoming show, contact the show secretary and obtain information
on the rules, regulations, and show standards.
As dwarf hamsters continue to grow in popu-
larity, more colors will be introduced and standards will change.

At most hamster shows, each hamster is
classed and judged with members of its own
species and sex. Categories are divided according to species, age, and coat color. There is a
conformation standard to describe each color
variety. Each hamster is awarded points according to how closely it matches the ideal standard. Body condition, eyes and ears, fur quality,
and how tame the pet is are all taken into consideration during the judging.

It is important to keep your pet in top shape.
Only show your hamster when it is at its best.
Who knows? Your efforts are about to pay off.
Make some room on that shelf. It's your turn
to bring home the trophy!

INFORMATION

Organizations

The American Society of Mammalogists
P.O. Box 1897
Lawrence, KS 66044
(785) 843-1235
(800) 627-0326
www.mammalsociety.org

American Veterinary Medical Association
1931 N. Meacham Road, Suite 100
Schaumberg, IL 60173-4360
(847) 925-8070
www.avma.org
E-mail: avmainfo@avma.org

National Academy of Sciences
500 Fifth Street
Washington, DC 20001
www.nasonline.org
E-mail: webmailbox@nas.edu

Hamster Clubs

California Hamster Association
www.geocities.com/CalHamAssoc
E-mail: calhamassoc@hotmail.com

Additional Reading
Magazines
Critters USA Annual Guide to Caring for Exotic Mammals. Irvine, CA: Fancy Publications.

Books
Bartlett, Patricia. *The Hamster Handbook* (Barron's Pet Handbooks). Hauppauge, NY: Barron's Educational Series, Inc. 2003.

Fritzsche, Peter. *My Hamster.* (My Pet Series). Hauppauge, NY: Barron's Educational Series, Inc., 2008.

Harkness, J. E., and J. E. Wagner. *The Biology and Medicine of Rabbits and Rodents.* London and Philadelphia: Lea and Febiger, 1989.

Hollmann, Peter. *My Hamster and Me* (For the Love of Animals). Hauppauge, NY: Barron's Educational Series, Inc., 2001.

Nowak, Ronald, ed. *Walker's Mammals of the World.* Baltimore and London: The Johns Hopkins University Press, 1999.

Percy, D. H., and S. W. Barthold. *Pathology of Laboratory Rodents and Rabbits.* Ames, IA: Iowa State University Press, 1993.

Ross, P. D. 1998. "Phodopus sungorus." *Mammalian Species,* 595: 1–9.

———. 1995. "Phodopus campbelli." *Mammalian Species,* 503: 1–7.

———. 1994. "Phodopus roborovskii." *Mammalian Species,* 459: 1–4.

Searle, A. G. *Comparative Genetics of Coat Colour in Mammals.* London: Logos Press Limited, 1967.

Siegal, H. I., ed. *The Hamster; Reproduction and Behavior.* New Brunswick, NJ: Rutgers University, 1985.

Stansfield, W. D. *Easy Outline of Genetics,* McGraw-Hill, 2002.

———. *Theory and Problems of Genetics,* 3rd Edition, McGraw-Hill, 1999.

Van Hoosier, G. L., and C. W. McPherson. *Laboratory Hamsters.* Orlando, FL: Academic Press, 1987.

INDEX

Important Note

This pet owner's guide tells the reader how to buy and care for dwarf hamsters. The advice given in the book applies to healthy animals with good dispositions obtained from a reputable source. Extraordinary efforts have been made by the author and the publisher to insure that treatment recommendations are precise and in agreement with standards accepted at the time of publication. If your hamster exhibits any signs of illness you should consult a veterinarian immediately—some diseases are dangerous for human beings. If you have any questions about an illness, or if you have been scratched or bitten by your hamster, consult a physician immediately. Some people are allergic to animal hair, dander, saliva, urine, and feces; are immune–suppressed; or are immunologically compromised, and cannot be exposed to animals. If you are not sure, consult your physician before you acquire a dwarf hamster.

Be sure to instruct children in the safe handling of dwarf hamsters and supervise children when they are handling dwarf hamsters. Never leave your pets or small children alone with dwarf hamsters.

If your hamster escapes, to prevent electrical accidents, be sure your hamster cannot gnaw on electrical wires and remember your hamster may cause you to fall if it runs between your feet and you are trying not to step on it.

The author and publisher assume no responsibility for and make no warranty with respect to results that may be obtained from procedures cited. Neither the author nor the publisher shall be liable for any damage resulting from reliance on any information contained herein, whether with respect to procedures, or by reason of any misstatement, error, or omission, negligent or otherwise, contained in this work. Information contained herein is presented as a reference only and is not a substitution for consultation with veterinarians or physicians.

The Author

Sharon Vanderlip, D.V.M. has a Bachelor of Science degree in Zoology from the University of California at Davis and a Doctor's degree in Veterinary Medicine. Dr. Vanderlip has provided veterinary care to exotic and domestic animal species for more than thirty years. She has written articles in peer-reviewed scientific publications and has authored twenty books on pet care. Dr. Vanderlip served as Clinical Veterinarian for the University of California at San Diego School of Medicine, conducted research with the Zoological Society of San Diego, is former Chief of Veterinary Services for the National Aeronautics and Space Administration (NASA), and has her own veterinary practice. Dr. Vanderlip has extensive experience with thousands of hamsters she has cared for during her veterinary career. Dr. Vanderlip may be contacted for seminars at *www.sharonvanderlip.com.*

Photo Credits

Animals Animals: 7, 8, 34, 44, 58, 61, 81, 82, 87, 88, 89 (top and bottom), 90. Lorraine Hill: 16 (bottom), 17, 69, 93, 97, 107. Zig Leszczynski: 4, 15, 25, 26, 29, 33, 41, 70, 79, 101. Shutterstock: 5, 47, 65, 94. Jacquelynn Vanderlip: 3, 6, 9, 16 (top), 21, 23, 24, 27, 28, 29, 35, 37, 38, 40, 45, 48, 50, 51, 52, 54, 55 (top and bottom), 59, 60, 63, 64, 68, 72, 73, 78, 91, 92, 98, 99, 100, 103, 104, 105. Sharon Vanderlip: 49, 85, 86.

Cover Photos

Front cover: Jacquelynn Vanderlip; back cover: Shutterstock; inside front cover and inside back cover: Zig Leszczynski.

Acknowledgments

A big thank you to my husband, Jack Vanderlip, D.V.M., for his assistance as an expert in laboratory and exotic animal medicine and for helping to obtain recent resources and new scientific information. Thanks also to our daughter, Jacquelynn, for all her help and cheerful enthusiasm. A lot has happened in the dwarf hamster world over the past decade and there were many exciting additions to include in this revision. Thanks to these two special people for freeing up time for me to revise this book!

All inquiries should be addressed to:
Barron's Educational Series, Inc.
250 Wireless Boulevard
Hauppauge, NY 11788
www.barronseduc.com

ISBN-13: 978-0-7641-4096-9
ISBN-10: 0-7641-4096-5

Library of Congress Control Number: 2008038868

Library of Congress Cataloging-in-Publication Data
Vanderlip, Sharon Lynn.
    Dwarf hamsters : everything about purchase, care, feeding, and housing / Sharon Vanderlip ; illustrations by Michele Earle-Bridges.
        p.   cm. — (A complete pet owner's manual)
    Includes bibliographical references and index.
    ISBN-13: 978-0-7641-4096-9 (alk. paper)
    ISBN-10: 0-7641-4096-5 (alk. paper)
    1. Dwarf hamsters as pets. I. Title.
    SF459.H3V36   2009
    636.935′6—dc22   2008038868

Printed in China
9 8 7 6 5 4 3 2 1